Essential Social Enterprise

a just transition to a regenerative fair future

Freer Spreckley

Social Enterprise is a means for individuals, families, and communities to take responsibility for their financial, social, and environmental wellbeing.

A Local Livelihoods publication
Local Livelihoods, The Slow House, Llandefalle,
Brecon LD3 0UN, Wales

www.locallivelihoods.com

This book is published by
Grosvenor House Publishing Ltd
Link House
140 The Broadway, Tolworth, Surrey, KT6 7HT.
www.grosvenorhousepublishing.co.uk

A CIP record for this book
is available from the British Library

ISBN 978-1-83975-706-8

I hope you find this publication of interest and helpful to the many thousands of people worldwide who have applied Social Enterprise ideas.

My thanks go to Camila Archer for her patient and diligent proofreading and editing, without which this publication would not be clear.

To my wife, Sally Spreckley, who has over many years supported me in developing the ideas and testing their accuracy in the ventures we have together created, I thank you dearly.

Contents

Preface

In many countries, Social Enterprise is known and supported without many people knowing what it is. This is not because of a lack of information; it is merely that Social Enterprise doesn't fit neatly into the current legal business models. Different people see Social Enterprise in different ways: for some, it's about non-profit volunteerism; for others, it's a for-profit commercial enterprise; for others again, it's all about social values, investment, and impact, or it can be seen as a multi-functional community enterprise. In some places, it's to do with responsible environmental action, and in other places it's to fulfil a social mission. In reality, it involves a paradigm shift from an old system of commercial business to a modern, relevant enterprise model.

Social Enterprise has inspired a change in the way people view the purpose and mission of today's organisations. It has led global companies and agencies towards a balanced approach to how they conceive their purpose or mission, and how they plan and measure performance. For commercial, public, and voluntary sector organisations, Social Enterprise has created the shift in thinking and practice from the single bottom line of profitability to the tripartite bottom line of financial viability, social wealth creation, and environmental responsibility.

In the late 1970s, Social Enterprise was developed as a definition of good practice in worker cooperatives and commercial organisations that adopted Social Accounting and Audit as part of their normative annual planning and performance measurement. Since the book 'Social Audit – A Management Tool for Co-operative Working' (1981) was published by Beechwood College, introducing Social Enterprise, the six values, and the tripartite planning and measurement method of Social Accounting and Audit, the concept has become shared and applied worldwide. In the original book, Social Enterprise was presented as a functional and structural organisational idea to complement and build on workers' cooperatives which are owned and democratically controlled by its workforce, and/or residents, if based within the geography of a community. Although the publication had a small print run of 2000 copies, and sold only in the UK and USA, its reach and impact has been profound.

The first to use the term Social Enterprise in any formal sense – other than ourselves at Beechwood College – was the DG VII Employment and Social Affairs Commission of the European Union. Beechwood College had submitted a proposal in 1980, under the Job Creation Programme, to run training courses for Social Enterprise and cooperatives. We were successful in attracting funding as part of their 'innovative criteria'. DG VII subsequently used the term in their publicity for some years, as part of their promotion of innovative examples and as a way to create jobs.

Social Enterprise was adopted by local development agencies, primarily funded by local authorities in the UK, to bolster their results in creating jobs via more traditional means. This happened specifically in 1998, when the London Workers Co-op Development Agency changed its name to the London Social Enterprise Agency. As people began to question what Social Enterprise really is, they began to understand that it was structurally like a workers' cooperative but with the additional criteria of social wealth creation and environmental responsibility. In the 1990s, in contrast to the 1970s, these two areas of concern were more prominent in the minds of politicians and activists alike. The London Social Enterprise Agency was able to renew itself, showing the way for Workers Co-op Agencies around the UK to become Social Enterprise Agencies without substantive change to their existing orthodoxy. It was a way to reinvigorate their movement and gain new life and funds.

For the first 20 years, up until the year 2000, Social Enterprise enjoyed a relative coherence by those involved in its structure and purpose. The term 'triple bottom line' was articulated in 1997 by John Elkington in a book entitled 'Cannibals With Forks: the triple bottom line of 21st-century business'. In the following years, social entrepreneurs took the values they liked, and discarded those they found challenging. Initially, the structure of Social Enterprise had six fundamental interlocking values. These got dislocated, and to some extent separated from each other, making subsectors out of particular values such as 'social value', 'social mission', monetising social accounting, or by substituting the word enterprise for the word business. Social value has become a specialist monitoring, evaluation, and impact subsector. Corporations have started adopting the triple bottom line as part of their Corporate Social Responsibility (CSR), and broadening their area of responsibilities.

Today, in many countries, the term Social Enterprise is sometimes used to pretend that the enterprise is more than the sum of its parts; that it has inherent and innate value irrespective of how it is structured and organised. When commercial profit dominates all thinking and actions, it is easy to confuse social wealth with social mission, and environmental responsibility can be overwhelmed by oceans of plastic waste.

In the US, the Social Enterprise Alliance was formed in 1998 as a national membership body; in India, since 2004 the Social Enterprises Academy has provided training; Social Traders in Australia was established in 2008. These are just a few examples of the global reach of Social Enterprise. Because these agencies' prime funded purpose was to create jobs, many of those involved shied away from defining Social Enterprise in any legal or structural way. Without a definition against which to examine the actual performance of Social Enterprises (or to test their legitimacy), the innovatory and revolutionary aspects were watered down. Critically, the definition and structure of ownership lost pace and excitement, whereas the concept of mission continued and flourished.

Social Enterprise is part of the solution to the challenge of fewer people owning assets and having control over their lives. The trend towards minority ownership has led to increasing commodification of many assets that were once in public ownership and free at the point of use. Public ownership and free use are mutually inclusive, as the interests of the public is the same as the interests of the individual user. Whereas the interests of the minority owner, who commodifies an asset and charges for its use, conflicts with the interests of the individual user who has previously had free access to use the asset. Had the original reasons for the creation of Social Enterprise diminished during the past 42 years, that would be that. However, the reasons have, unfortunately, become much more urgent and have reinforced its original justification. The fundamental problems have deepened, and affected larger numbers of people.

The world we now live in has outgrown the structures of business that pursue growth exclusively and at any costs, as the only mission of purpose. No longer 'where there's muck there's brass', but in its place for the 21st-century 'where there's trade and shared ownership there's wellbeing'. Can the world afford to support multinational organisations that continue to appropriate resources, skills, and energy, and the natural environment for their profits? The trend to amalgamate ever smaller entities – both public and private – into single larger bodies results in excluding new entrants' ability to gain assets. The bigger the entity, the less likely it is that people will have the means to be involved and to obtain benefits. Monopolistic asset ownership leads increasingly to more people finding themselves disenfranchised and powerless. All around us, there is an incremental cost of basic amenities for tax-paying people. At the same time, we see huge corporations getting away without paying taxes on their enormous net profits.

Where institutions are extractive, they exercise power with few constraints, allowing the proprietor ultimate control over the business, the employees, the use of resources, and the generation of waste. In the face of emotional and physical injustice, it is harder for people to care for the natural environment on which we depend. Communities continue butting up against each other, and new industrial and agricultural developments, precipitated by economic, social, and environmental migration, result in friction, fear and, in some cases, war. Simultaneously, society is accelerating technological and scientific development, which challenge our understanding and ethics. Science is racing ahead of human structures of governance. Many commentators point out that soon science will overtake the human brain in deciding the future. The owners of the technology's intellectual property rights will also own society and the future.

Types of commercial organisation able to incorporate more sensitive interpretations and definitions of viability and complex responsibilities are thus urgently needed as a counterweight to the existing narrow forms of corporate governance. Social Enterprise is inclusive and regenerative; the integration of human, physical, and natural resources, creates the point when mutual benefit occurs, sparking greater efficiency and innovation, and is liberal in enabling members to apply democratic control and achieve more extensive human benefits. Could regenerative forms of organisation which are viable in their own right also be a catalyst for creative destruction of the old narrow approach?

Social Enterprise's revolutionary contribution to society lies in the way it redefines organisational viability – what it means to be successful and facilitates active involvement in shared ownership, decision making, and governance by large numbers of people. Viability, in the 21st century, cannot be left to the detrimental idea of financial profit maximisation. It is inconsistent to support a globally interconnected society and be responsible for the finite resources of the planet. Social Enterprise can spearhead human rights and social inclusion in a real and practical way. The exploration of and experimentation with these new organisational systems is vital towards overcoming the monumental financial, social, and environmental problems that are stacking up around the world.

At the very core of society is the lawful right of ownership. Ownership rights underpin our current systems; every individual has such rights, and to advocate an alternative is unthinkable. The real purpose of Social Enterprise is to address the fundamental issues of inequality, by enabling workers to own and control their enterprises, and fashion an organisation that is regenerative in all its operations, rather than to ease the conscience of those who want to own and control, and set the social mission for others to carry out. In respect of a new business model, intentionality is essential. People have to want to be involved in the responsibilities and work of a Social Enterprise. Once Social Enterprises and communities own land, buildings, intellectual rights, and machinery, once labour hires capital and owns assets, alternative ways of creating wellbeing become possible. As I said many years ago, in Social Enterprise, the main change is from a legal right of 'capital hiring labour to labour hiring capital'. This fundamental change is achievable using existing company law, the free market economic system, local and national democracy. People don't just have to have a job to earn income – indeed, both how people 'earn' and what constitutes 'income' will have to change. How they share the work and gain the fruits of these resources will become the innovation.

Social Enterprise is emblematic of the need for global change. The significant positive feature today is that Social Enterprise is good business. Customers, traders, banks, and public authorities want to trade with Social Enterprises as long as they can prove their performance against the Triple Bottom Line and the ownership and democratic structure are transparent. I do not doubt in my mind that the tripartite values of Social Enterprise will come to form the global benchmark against which public, private, and community-based organisations plan and measure their performance. Now that we have these values, they are not only obvious, but how can they not be included?

This is relevant because democracy is under attack. Critics state that it is not that efficient, and it is perhaps time to reappraise how society manages its affairs. They cite China as an example of efficiency, and even dare to suggest we in the West can find some middle ground between democracy and autocracy. Instead of running away from democracy and back into some medieval state of feudalism or political populism, we must strengthen democracy and make it more relevant to an enlightened society. Democracy is inherently progressive, as it frees thinking and invites – from the broadest group of people – ideas, critiques, and learning, necessary for a society that balances efficiency with social and human dignity through self-management. For Social Enterprise to flourish and be part of the solution, as an alternative to corporate and private business, it needs a clear definition.

The addition of the three critical areas of performance measurement – financial viability, social wealth creation, and environmentally responsible action – as criteria to plan, measure, and account for the operational performance, is the significant contribution of Social Enterprise. The Social Accounting and Audit system designed for Social Enterprise is the engine to drive change.

This book lays out the history, foundation, and definition of Social Enterprise: the relationship between human behaviour and the six values needed for inclusive and regenerative institutions in the 21st century. Above all, it attempts to make the case that Social Enterprise is part of a change for a just transition to a regenerative fair future, moving across from social and economic injustice and the climate catastrophe brought about by the unfettered growth of the global neoliberal economic system. Society needs a new business model for our age, where financial equality, human wellbeing, and environmentally responsible behaviours are the structures upon which trade is conducted.

1 INTRODUCING A NEW IDEA

Innovative ideas usually originate in the minds of individuals or small groups; they rarely originate from corporate or institutional research. It takes freedom of thought and freedom of constraints to think through to new ideas. It takes a considerable leap to jettison existing principles and come up with new ones at the same time. In institutions, a cross-section of representatives in the group has to agree to give up something traditional and replace it with something new. It takes courage to stick your neck out and advocate for something unknown or previously unheard of.

In the late 1970s, I developed the concept of and a primary method for, conducting a regular internal Social Accounting and Audit procedure.[1] This was the first internal method for organisations to plan and measure performance against a set of non-commercial values, and in response to how stakeholders viewed the behaviour of the organisations' operations. The primary motivation came from the fact that traditional cooperative movement, the world over, was in trouble and decline. I surmised that cooperatives had lost sight of their initial seven principles and had, in effect, just become another type of business, albeit a bit unwieldy. This led, in 1978, to the idea of using three criteria to measure business performance, the Social Accounting and Audit system, and the term Social Enterprise. In 1981, I wrote a short book entitled 'SOCIAL AUDIT – A Management Tool for

---

[1] Up to this time, Social Audit was a known procedure used as a one-off external investigation. Our approach at Beechwood College was to internalise it and integrate it as part of the regular internal planning and measurement procedure alongside financial auditing

1

Co-operative Working', setting out the reasons and methods for existing cooperatives to incorporate these ideas in planning and measuring their trading performance.

The seven principles that the Rochdale Pioneers developed in 1844 were created to unify and define new values by which to govern and own businesses. Some of these were adopted worldwide; for example, universal children's education; some are now out of date, and political change had superseded others. Customers own their cooperatives as members who all share in the profits in the form of dividends received annually – known as the 'divi'. The divi has been adopted and adapted by major supermarket groups as the 'loyalty card', but without the democratic ownership and control by customers. It seemed to me that for cooperatives to refocus on their core principles, these principles needed to be part of their annual planning and review at the time, but cooperatives were only planning and reviewing their commercial and financial operations. Their extra-commercial purpose, in contrast, became devoid of social content. To make cooperatives relevant, I suggested that, in addition to common ownership and democratic governance, they should have three core principles or values - financial viability, social wealth creation, and environmental responsibility – and, by implication, move on from the original seven principles that are, in essence, a list of activities. Alongside this, the cooperatives should systematically plan, apply, and measure their operations against these three operational core values as part of their annual management planning and review cycle. In this way, they would keep their values relevant and in plain sight, making the values part of the everyday management and operations, so that they would have a genuine and real impact.

However, the question was: is the term cooperative still relevant to the type of business I was describing? The motivation for creating a new term for cooperatives was threefold. Firstly, cooperatives in the UK had become indistinguishable from other supermarket business and had, so it seemed, jettisoned any pretence to the ideals of their socialist past. During the 1970s, the cooperative stores were in free fall, with many cooperative societies folding and merging as individual stores closed down in response to competition from new capitalist rivals. The traditional cooperative movement lacked the management expertise to compete with the private sector supermarkets. Secondly, cooperatives in many developing countries had been taken over by the State, mostly at the time of independence from their colonial invaders, and run as nationalised public enterprises masquerading as cooperatives. They continued relying on individual farmer members to supply the raw material, at low prices and with slow payments, for cash crop exports. In many cases, they no longer functioned as cooperatives: in the mid-1980s, agencies such as the United Nations ceased support for organisations that had the word 'cooperative' in their title, as part of the neoliberal agenda driven by Thatcher and Reagan. Thirdly, I felt that if Social Accounting and Audit was to become real and an alternative to the single criteria of profit maximisation, then the organisations using the method needed a new identity, even a new name – one that defined their purpose better. The Social Accounting and Audit method was designed for cooperatives which were already under common ownership and democratic governance, to distinguish them from those who only measured performance using the financial bottom line. But what to call them?

I held many discussions with colleagues and friends about the term Social Enterprise; the term combined apparently contradictory meanings of 'social' and 'enterprise'. It went through several iterations in my mind before I started to use the term, and before going public with the idea. The term had no previous incarnation, as far as I could see, and because it was an intentional oxymoron, it proved memorable and inclusive. So, the term Social Enterprise was coined at Beechwood College during the late 1970s, and later incorporated into the book 'SOCIAL AUDIT – A Management Tool for Co-operative Working' (1981). Beechwood College was a worker cooperative, which ran a college and conference centre in Leeds, UK, that had been set up with support from the Industrial Common Ownership Movement (ICOM). We firmly aligned with the principles of worker cooperatives as employee-owned and controlled commercial enterprises. Workers cooperatives, at the time, were experiencing a renaissance, due to the work of ICOM sponsoring a UK government Private Members' Bill in Parliament to create the Industrial Common Ownership Act 1976, and formulating a set of model rules. At the time, I was an executive member of ICOM. I sat on the worker cooperative sub-committee, so was intimately involved in shepherding the ICO Act through Parliament and developing the new model rules. From this experience, I learned a lot about politics. While the model rules enabled worker cooperatives to secure registration quickly, they were nonetheless grappling with the balance between democratic governance and commercial business. To add additional criteria and responsibility was considered by many people involved in politics to be a step too far. So, it was with regret that I ventured out into the territory of Social Enterprise and Social Accounting and Audit on my own, without the backing of ICOM or the Co-operative Movement to which Beechwood College was politically aligned.

Many academics and writers wonder how Social Enterprise and the three criteria of financial, social, and environmental values became so popular. I think they find it difficult to imagine such a big idea coming from such a small place, but big ideas do come from little individuals when they have no baggage and no internal constraints. However, the influences I had received to reach this point and develop the idea were numerous and vital.

My understanding of democratic structures was forged early: at school. I became a boarding pupil at Summerhill School in 1954, the place run by A.S Neill, which was the first free school. Children and staff conducted the affairs of the school, and democratically made all decisions at weekly meetings. Everything was discussed and voted on, from big issues about smoking and bedtimes to less essential matters about looking after the chickens, or if we could ride our bikes indoors or not. We never discussed or voted on attending lessons – they were always optional. No kid was going to vote in favour of compulsory attendance at lessons, so there was no-one to bring up such a subject at meetings. A pupil always chaired the weekly Saturday night meeting of around 70 kids and 15 adults. The role of the chair rotated every week, so many kids got to be the chair – that way we learned respect for the position of chair and how to behave in meetings. Because every child attended the meetings (it was the culture and not compulsory), we discussed everything, and all knew about everything that was going on in the school. We had all been involved in the decision-making – the democracy made Summerhill transparent and feel safe.

I learned that democracy is good fun, efficient, and engenders a sense of equality, camaraderie, and trust. The participation by children and adults together creates cultural behaviour that translates, over time and trial and error, into values. In the nine years I spent as a pupil at Summerhill School, I learned the art of democracy (don't cry when you lose, don't laugh when you win, enjoy the camaraderie and the extraordinarily efficient and decent way to run society).

Other influences also caused me to venture into alternative ways of viewing the world. My father David was trained at the Royal Military Academy Sandhurst, and graduated as a cavalry officer who became a conscientious objector before the Second

World War. This so infuriated his family that he was disowned and disinherited, and lost his current and future wealth for the principle of pacifism. He was a founder of the concept of wholefoods, developed in 1946 at Goosegreen Farm – an intentional community in Somerset – by the group of pioneering pacifists who moved to the country at the end of the war. Their purpose was to start growing food organically and living frugally, and later he became an early member, in the 1950s, of the Conservation Society (one of the early environmental groups in the UK), was a lifelong organic gardener, and a founding member of the Industrial Common Ownership Movement (ICOM).

My experience with cooperatives and common ownership goes back to the late 1960s, when my father started to convert his company from a privately-owned business into an employee-owned enterprise, called Landsmans Co-ownership Ltd. The process of converting the company was a long, drawn-out affair, involving lots of research, meetings, experts coming and going, and staff being apprehensive and unsure of what it meant for their jobs. It is true to say that some of the workers, who were to end up owning the company, never really trusted my father; they couldn't understand why he would want to give the company away. Although I was young and not involved, nonetheless the process took place in our house, and I, of course, listened in. I learned from his humility and quiet strength. For the second time in his life, he had knowingly given up his wealth, as he no longer owned the company he set up. What I learned from this is the need to build trust. If people don't trust change, it will be compromised, opposed, and weakened. The full involvement of all concerned must be paramount as an open and transparent process.

After leaving school in 1963, and working on a building site until I left home at 17 years old, I hitchhiked around the world, briefly returning in 1970 a wiser person. During my travels, I visited 82 countries, mostly hitchhiking from one side of the country to the other, often staying in the capital city for some time, and visiting known sites of interest, and some of the less well known. Hitchhiking, eating fruit and street food, and sleeping rough in rural areas under trees and bushes, and in building sites and urban crevasses in towns and cities, meant I was living for less than £1 a day. It was during this time that I encountered structural poverty in India: purposely designed and executed. I remember standing one early morning in a Victorian wrought iron indoor market in Calcutta, piled high with pyramids of food. I was standing admiring the symmetry of the fruit piles, when shuffling around the bottom of one of the concrete plinths, on which the fruit was piled high, came a small figure who was pushing himself along on a plywood plank with what looked like roller-skate wheels nailed to the underside. With his hands, which were bound in rubber made from car tyres, he pushed himself along towards me, and twirled a complete circle and stopped at my feet. His legs were twisted and wrapped around his waist, he was only the size of his upper body, small and thin with long, glossy jet black, wavy hair. And as he looked up at me, an enormous smile, full of gleaming white teeth, came across his face as he put out his hand and begged for something in the midst of plenty. It is likely his parents broke his bones and tied his limbs to mend as a disabled person when he was a baby, to enhance his chances of success as an adult beggar. He held out his hand as he came towards me, with a smile as a professional function. My immediate thought and lesson were that if structural poverty can be engineered, as in the beggar's case, then structural wellbeing, it must follow, can also be engineered. If we can harness fire, learn to talk, create agriculture, build the pyramids, go to the moon, and invent artificial intelligence, surely we can engineer civil society to be full of wellbeing.

In 1971/2, during the war of independence in Bangladesh, I returned to India as a member of Operation Omega – a nonviolent action group working with the Gandhi Peace Foundation in Calcutta (now Kolkata), set up to inform the British public about the plight of millions of refugees fleeing the civil war in East Pakistan. We undertook Satyagraha (nonviolent direct action) by sitting down at the Bangladesh/India border, demonstrating against the war, got arrested, released, and did it again. I visited the interior of East Pakistan/Bangladesh as part of a contingent of Freedom Fighters (Mukti Bahini) on one of their forays into Bangladesh when fighting the Pakistani army. I realised that there was a widespread cholera epidemic in rural communities. Cholera was the big killer at the time, so I left Operation Omega and set up an organisation called the Cholera Cure Unit. This was supported financially by the Catholic Bishop of Calcutta, on the proviso that I used my ex-army ambulance to help Mother Teresa ferry goods and people for her mission under the Howrah Bridge in the centre of the city. This was my first experience of setting up an organisation. The CCU, as it became known, extended the work of several American and Bengali doctors based in the refugee camps around Calcutta. There were estimated to be 10 million refugees, who had fled into India from East Pakistan to escape the war, get hold of food and, importantly, medical supplies.

Up to that point, the only cure for cholera was an intravenous solution that was unavailable and impossible to administer in rural communities during a civil war. I organised groups of young student doctors from the refugee camps to be trained by the American doctors, who were pioneering the oral rehydration method and who were administering it in the refugee camps, but not in the rural areas. I arranged to trek with the Freedom Fighters, taking groups of student doctors and longboats or bullock cartloads of the dry rehydration ingredients, and set up cholera cure clinics in rural areas deep inside Bangladesh.

The CCU also provided information on how to create an oral rehydration solution from the four necessary ingredients, as a self-help component of the work. The Cholera Cure Units were successful in enabling local communities to self-administer the oral rehydration solution, and proved the value of the method without there being medical staff on hand. By the end of the war, the success of using oral rehydration to combat cholera started to become an accepted method for countering dehydration in general; today, its impact is felt worldwide. It is now available in just about any chemist in the world.

The lesson for me was: it's not so much what you know, but the willingness to do it, which counts. I had no experience in health, project management, or fundraising, but because of the need, these were quickly overcome. The will to do is more vital than the knowledge of how to do it, and from then on, for me imagining new ideas and setting up new ventures became achievable.

After the liberation of East Pakistan in 1972, and during the formation of the new country known as Bangladesh, I spent time in Dhaka advocating for village cooperatives and rural credit unions as part of the new economy for Bangladesh. I learned a lot about rural cooperatives and how to reinvigorate and regenerate old institutions.

One event which gave me an insight into the future world, occurred when hitchhiking across Africa from the Congo to Tanzania. The guard stopped me at the border between Kenya and Tanzania for wearing bell-bottom trousers. Bell-bottom fashions were outlawed by the Tanzanian government at that time, to protect their youth from Western influence. So, I asked the border guard whether he would let me in if I sewed them up. 'Yes,' he said. I walked back to a small village, through where a railway track ran, and sat down in a café, ordered tea, and sewed up my bell-bottom trousers so they became straight trousers. While sewing, I became aware of a commotion far off in the distance from the café. I was in no hurry, so spent some time there watching the commotion move slowly towards the café. As it got nearer, I could see four men holding a large tarpaulin on four poles. Smoke was billowing out from all sides, and the noise of raking gravel, banging of metal on metal, and quick-fire chatter in a foreign language could just about be heard. The whole din was inching along in unison, like a large, noisy, smoky machine. As it got nearer, I could make out lots of men shovelling gravel, banging steel pegs fixing railway sleepers to the ground, and then carrying large railway lines into place and pegging them. All the men were chain-smoking, and the four pole holders slowly moved the whole tarpaulin along to protect the men from the blazing East African sun. They were chattering in Chinese and laying a new railway line. There were no Tanzanians around, and this was China in control in Africa. I marvelled at the intensity of the men's work, the synchronised working pattern, and the authority being meted out by the individual sitting on a chair. I recognised that I had never seen people work like that before, and most definitely not in England. I had previously been to China in 1966, and witnessed the multitudes going about their business, and thought that if these people worked like that they would become the world leaders, and no-one could stop them. Many years later, I was having a conversation with a businessman in the UK and relayed this story, explaining that I thought the Chinese would overtake the West in the next couple of decades. He insisted that it would take 100 years for the Chinese to catch up with the West. My lesson was to believe in what you're seeing, and don't trust Western business people who have no experience of seeing the future, and worse, who still base their commercial plans on racial bias.

Because I had spent six years hitchhiking around the world and had not been interested in making money, or spending it, I had managed to see so many places, meet lots of fantastic people, visit some of the world's most celebrated attractions, and a lot more besides. I had little money, and always stayed in hot climate countries, sleeping rough every night, eating fruit and cheap local street food, and meeting the thousands of drivers who generously gave me lifts. I had had a unique experience, not available to those with money who would have caught the bus or plane and stayed in hotels and talked only to taxi drivers and hotel receptionists.

In 1974, nine years after first leaving home, I set up a commune called Lifespan. With a good friend, Hylda Sims, we bought 19 ex-railway workers' terraced houses in the South Yorkshire moors, just outside Barnsley, and invited people to come and join us to live in a commune. Thirty-five adults and three children joined within the first few months. It was all about learning to live a different lifestyle where we shared resources, work, income, and managed the commune through a weekly meeting, where everyone had one vote. Many of the original methods we used at Lifespan reflected both Hylda's and my experience of being pupils of Summerhill School. We formed a legal constitution that specified members are residents who have lived in the commune for more than six weeks, and that members automatically ceased being a member once they have stopped being a resident for more than six weeks. Everyone was a member and owner of the land and buildings, and had one vote in every meeting. Lifespan still works as a community, and still has the same type of legal and management structure today, some 46 years later.

The long-term survival of Lifespan is undoubtedly to do with the resilience of its members, and also its constitution. The constitution drawn up in 1978 was fit for the 21st century, with its common ownership and democratic structure. And it's more inclusive values of social, environmental, and financial aims have stood the test of time for its relevance to today's global and local challenges. Because the 35 adults and three kids all shared the resources, the economics were viable, and the living was comfortable, and we didn't need or receive any State aid.

While working in the commune's wholefood shop in Huddersfield one day, I was serving two older women who were reminiscing about how their mothers' cooked black peas, when a motorcycle policeman entered. I could see the women thought he was after me – I was a bit of a hippy at the time – but he chatted about how nutritious the food in the shop was, and bought quite a lot. On his way out, the policeman said to one of the women, who had a box of cornflakes in her basket, that there was 'more nutrition in the cardboard box than in the cornflakes'. Only that week, our accountant had suggested that the wholefood shop was bankrupt, as it didn't make enough money to pay decent salaries, never mind a profit. He was right, but as the policeman had implied, the value was in the nutrition not in the profit. I reflected on the notion of 'value', as at that time we at the commune were interested in nutrition, not profit; we didn't need profit, but we did need good health, as we were self-producers.

We ran several community enterprises, and made a financial profit in some of them and a loss in others. Yet, all were of value, as far as we were concerned, but value in a different sense than purely financial profit. It occurred to me that the accountant and his emphasis on financial auditing shouldn't be the only way we determine value; we needed new notions of value within trading organisations, and additional methods of measuring value. Lifespan's experience showed clearly that the economics of sharing is eminently superior to single ownership and use. Sharing combines benefits in terms of cost reductions, personal interaction, having access to a wide range of tools and equipment, and reducing pressure on finite resources.

In the 1970s, the rising impact of financial inequality, the lack of real democracy, and the environmental damage and cost of overuse of resources, were all becoming well understood by the poor urban and rural populations who bore the brunt of climate change. Citizens went to the voting booths at every election, but could not see or experience benefits they thought their vote would usher in. As global pollution and essential utilities became visibly worse, and things like clean drinking water became scarcer in some countries, it was clear that those who now – and in the future – would experience the worst effects, were those who owned nothing and had no money: the poor people of the world.

Alternative values needed to be developed that countered the old-fashioned view of the single bottom line of financial profit as the only criteria used to measure commercial performance. This was clearly inadequate, and although there was little idea of alternatives, I at least felt that new values, in addition to structural change, were needed. I discussed this idea with two friends, Tony Naughton, a chartered accountant, and John Fryer, a lawyer who specialised in corporate and charitable law. They both assured me that it would be straightforward to prepare social and ecological criteria that met the UK's Generally Accepted Accounting Practice (GAAP) specifications, and that could be inserted and registered within a legal constitution of a trading company.

Growing the Idea

Worker cooperatives had a short-lived and impactful revival in the 1970s, spurred on by ICOM's model rules that were prepared to support the Industrial Common Ownership Act 1976. At this point, ICOM only had 13 member companies, who were all common ownership or co-ownership companies, and most had converted from being a conventional private sector business to a common ownership employee-governed enterprise.

At the same time as ICOM was developing their model rules, in the UK groups of young people were setting up 'alternative collectives', creating new enterprises in wholefoods, bookshops, printing, and renewable energy. These groups were mostly unincorporated, and were trading as collectives. In law, they were sole traders, or partnerships with no limited liability cover that made them vulnerable to personal liability. The biggest group of these collectives in the UK was the wholefood shops and warehouses in the North of England. There existed in 1976 over a hundred shops that formed themselves into the Federation of Northern Wholefood Collectives. They would meet regularly to discuss and learn from each other, and attempt to define and understand the root meaning and origin of wholefoods. We also discussed supply chains, and how to equalise receipts by all those involved from the producers in developing countries to the retailers in the UK. At that time, wholefoods were a new type of food, and we spent much time talking about how to encourage more people to buy and, importantly, how to cook them.

It was at one of the Northern Wholefood Collective's gatherings at Lifespan Commune when the Wholefood Collectives and the ICOM Model Rules were introduced to each other. The Wholefood Collectives were searching for suitable legal structures for their enterprise, and the ICOM rules seemed a perfect fit. Over the next year, more than a hundred Wholefood Collectives, not just from the North of England, used the ICOM Model Rules to register their collectives as worker cooperatives, and ICOM's membership grew to over two hundred firms from a base of 13 in little more than two years.

Unfortunately, in 1977, the Northern Wholefood Collective disbanded itself. Although the individual shops continued to thrive, and the warehouse, Suma Wholefoods Cooperative that was at the heart of the broader collective, also thrived and prospered, the politics of workers cooperatives suffered. The reason for disbanding was significant: one of the initiatives undertaken by the collective had been to raise a 1% levy of net profits from all the shops and warehouse. This was voluntary, and it hardly made a difference to the viability of the cooperatives, as each one contributed a small amount. At one meeting, the treasurer announced that over £7,000 had been collected so far, and perhaps we should think of how this could be used. Most of us had no idea we had collected such a large sum in a short time. After about an hour of discussion, it was plain that we had quite different ideas for how to use the money, and had no sort of common ground. Because we were talking about the present and not the future, the money was tantalisingly close; we could write a cheque right there and then. So, after a further half-hour, and getting nowhere near an agreement, someone jokingly suggested that if we couldn't agree, let's give the money back to the shops. Without much ado, this went to a vote and easily won. To this day, I am mystified as to the motivation for this vote. But what I did learn was that when it comes to deciding how to spend profit or surplus money, it is best to do so before it has been made. Deciding on how to distribute surplus should be part of a strategic discussion. The outcome of this decision was the main reason for the demise of the Northern Wholefood Collective. It just took the wind out of our sails; it was the biggest action of the collectives, and in a single moment of collective madness, we abounded our finest achievement. The Federation had focused on developing the 1% levy and collecting the money; we had not thought about how to spend it, or what we might do with the fund. The lesson was for organisations to plan and use strategy to formulate policy to help make operational decisions.

In 1978, when I left Lifespan and moved to Leeds to set up Beechwood College as a learning centre for worker cooperatives, I started to develop the mechanism for how to structure Social Accounting and Audit alongside financial auditing. One of the reasons for moving and setting up Beechwood College was that Lifespan had become too inward-looking for my liking. I seemed the only person there interested in being involved in external networks of like-minded organisations. The move to Beechwood allowed me to re-engage in the broader questions of organisational development – what type of organisations do we want, and who and what should they serve?

With my experience of Lifespan, Summerhill School, the Indian caste system, and ICOM, it seemed to me that as a civil society, we organise virtually everything intentionally, from our weekly shopping list and grocery purchases to global monopolies and multinational representative bodies. Therefore, we are capable of fashioning organisations any way we like within the existing legal system, and even that, through the right channels, can be changed and re-organised. There was no reason we could not re-engineer and structure commercial organisations to serve society's needs in the 20th/21st centuries – not the 19th century, as was then and still is today's business model.

The process of developing Social Enterprise and Social Accounting and Audit was incremental. For some time at Beechwood, we ran seminars and training workshops on Social Accounting and Audit, and promoted the idea with larger conferences. The book: "SOCIAL AUDIT – A Management Tool for Co-operative Working" came out at the same time, and introduced the tripartite planning and measurement criteria, the Social Accounting and Audit system, and the term Social Enterprise. The book sold well, and we had to order two reprints in my time. We had successfully submitted a proposal to the

European Commission, under their Job Creation Programme, to run a three-year training and development programme for Social Enterprises and worker cooperatives. Subsequently, the Commission's DG VIII Directorate-General for Development, Employment, and Social Affairs, which ran the funding streams, started to use the term Social Enterprise as an example of one of their funded innovatory programmes. This had been our innovative component for a successful funding bid; the concept had taken hold, and moved beyond our network into the European Union.

During the 1990s and up to the present time, Social Enterprise has continued to grow organically from within existing development agencies around the world. The early 1990s saw the London Co-operative Development Agency (CDA) change its name to Social Enterprise London. This happened at a series of workshops facilitated by Jim Brown, who had been our lead trainer at Beechwood College, and had picked up the idea of Social Enterprise while there. Academic institutions and individuals also started to enquire about and investigate the concept of Social Enterprise and Social Accounting and Audit. Cliff Southcombe and I set up Social Enterprise Partnership Ltd in 1993, to provide training and consultancy to new groups forming enterprises. Cliff has continued to work in the Social Enterprise sector ever since, through Social Enterprise Europe. A few multinational support bodies, such as the British Council and the European Union EuropeAid programme, continue to support Social Enterprise.

Since those early days, I have continued to support and work in Social Enterprise, mainly as a team member of consultancy companies, and as a freelance consultant and trainer. During this period, I have worked for multilateral and bilateral agencies, national government ministries, and local community organisations and Social Enterprises in 66 countries.

Mainly, the work has been in restructuring and competency, strengthening ministries and departments to build capacity, supporting Social Enterprise and other development areas. In support of the restructuring work, I have worked in the design and implementation of programmes, monitoring and impact analysis, and advising independent organisations on how to apply Social Accounting and Audit systems. This work has also included writing manuals on Social Enterprise, Social Accounting and Audit, and in Results-Based Management. Being involved in development work has been tremendously rewarding. I have learnt many new techniques and organisational systems that I have adopted and incorporated into updated Social Enterprise methods. Specifically, the Logical Framework way of preparing plans is now used in preparation for the Social Accounting and Audit method.

More recently, national and international organisations, such as Social Value UK, Social Audit Network, and B Corp, have become membership and training networks focusing on different methods of Social Accounting and Audit. There have also been attempts at setting up a social stock exchange in Europe and India. Several social impact investment vehicles and peer-to-peer lending schemes are also active in financial services. In the area of legal structures, we still have cooperative societies, workers cooperatives, housing cooperatives, and in the UK the Employee Ownership Association (a direct offshoot of ICOM). In addition to those organisations which directly support commercial companies to become more socially and environmentally aware, there is also the emergence of community-based development along the lines of community enterprise. This is used as a way for local groups to form community-owned and democratically governed enterprises, to become more self-reliant and independent of external funders and local government. Higher education institutes are also incorporating Social Enterprise in the curriculum and research.

As an indication of the level of commitment to commercial organisations, many of the supporting agencies competed with each other for both ideas on the correct interpretation and in attracting paying members. The global rallying cry of people, planet, and profit – the three pillars of sustainable development used by the United Nations – was becoming a crucial universal criterion for measuring performance in government, NGOs, and private sector enterprises. Social Enterprise had caught the imagination of many people looking for alternative methods of structuring and managing businesses.

However, the inability, in the UK, to agree a shared Social Enterprise definition has had a marked detrimental impact on the growth and strength of the sector. Since the late 1970s, when the concept of Social Enterprise was first invented, many interpretations and terms have been applied. This has confused commentators, policymakers, and politicians, and in my opinion has hindered Social Enterprise potential. Muddled thinking has frustrated those wishing to support and those wishing to use the model to set up their enterprises. Social Enterprise has directly spawned many offshoots, and indirectly given a boost to existing social economy organisations, to such an extent that it is correct to say that it has engendered a new system of social economy initiatives. But, without a definition, Social Enterprise is in danger of imploding through a lack of clarity and courage.

2 THE POPULARITY OF SOCIAL ENTERPRISE; OR WHEN WE ALL GOT CONFUSED

Social Enterprise, in its core sense, is a beautiful reflection of humanness. It contains the fundamental right of ownership, participation in society affairs, self-determination, self-esteem, financial independence, and free interaction with fellow citizens of all countries: key tenets of human rights.

Social Enterprise and social entrepreneurship emerged at about the same time (Social Enterprise in 1978 at Beechwood College, as part of the workers' cooperative movement; the social entrepreneurship movement emerged within a project called Ashoka in the US in 1980), and it is fair to say that they have both compromised each other and benefited each other. A more thorough analysis would be needed to determine precisely the costs and benefits of that relationship.

Social Enterprise had, from the very beginning, a definition of being a common ownership enterprise, democratically governed with financial, social, and environmental objectives as its core purpose. Social entrepreneurship, on the other hand, is a term defining 'a person who pursues novel applications that have the potential to solve community-based problems'; it refers not to an organisation, but individuals' behaviour. A social entrepreneur could, for example, set up a playgroup, a Social Enterprise, a community project, or a business that has social aims. Social entrepreneurship is clearly to do good works, but is clouded in confusion, as there have always been individuals who have done good works or been active in social projects. In Victorian times in the UK, many people set up social welfare trusts: might these today be called social entrepreneurs? In many countries, there are hundreds of thousands of people who volunteer locally to set up and run projects providing free services to people in need.

The UK's Labour Government (1997-2007) created a vague and misleading definition, 'A Social Enterprise is a business with primarily social objectives whose surpluses are principally reinvested for that purpose in the business or in the community, rather than being driven by the need to maximise profit for shareholders and owners.'[2] Although this statement reflects half of a Social Enterprise definition, it was used widely in the UK and internationally, and as a consequence, become believable and stuck in the literature. This definition is so watered down as to be meaningless, but that did not stop it being used by the development agencies, both national and regional, and by academics who wrote scholarly articles on Social Enterprise. In reality, the DTI's definition can equally apply to Social Enterprise and social entrepreneurship. But, because they are different, it only made things worse, by compromising each other's purpose and not illustrating what these new types of organisation represent.

Lurking behind this definition is a sop to those, like me, who advocated for a bold and clear definition, and a bit of hoodwinking to those who want change without having to make an effort. Having one definition for two types of ideas, with similar sounding terms, meant that for many years Social Enterprise and social entrepreneurship were used interchangeably in the same paragraph in written material and presentations, so that they, seemingly, became the same thing. Both terms have found favour with governments, financial institutions, and development

---

[2]   Source: Social Enterprise: A Strategy for Success (DTI, 2002)

agencies, and because the definitions have been undefined, for many they are indistinguishable, thus allowing for misuse and confusion of both terms.

While there are many genuine Social Enterprises and many hundreds of thousands of individuals who do good work, the net result is that there are so many organisations calling themselves Social Enterprise that the term has become empty. On the positive side, the vagueness of the term has enabled many people to 'have a go' at being a social entrepreneur that, had they used the real definition, would not have entered into the more socially responsible businesses. Social Enterprise is now known as 'doing good', and I'm sure most of these ventures do try to do good. Over time, how they fare is less well known. Do they focus less on their social and environmental mission and slowly drop the 'social' in their business altogether? Or do they find that actually running it as a Social Enterprise is the same, and good business? As most of these companies don't report by using a form of social auditing, it is difficult to know.

Two well-known companies, the Body Shop in the UK and Ben and Jerrys in the USA, found that having, and reporting on, their social mission was good for business. They both applied social auditing in their annual reports, although neither company ever converted to a common ownership structure, nor, indeed, included in their Social Audit any questions on how staff felt about the company. There was no internal assessment, just a focus on their contribution to social causes. Of course, both companies subsequently sold themselves to larger corporations, with the individual founders pocketing the vast sums of money received and the workers just being moved to new owners.

Social Enterprise is defined, but in many countries differently interpreted, while social entrepreneurship is undefined and used by many to mask their real structure and behaviour. Yet the confusion between Social Enterprise and social entrepreneurship creates a flexible situation. The options are much greater, and consequently, more people find something to suit them, so there are more social initiatives that look good. Still, if they are just private business dressed up as a social venture, there is no positive impact. Even worse, the ambiguity engenders long-term damage to the whole social economy sector. Yes, sometimes it isn't easy to know if this is merely a marketing technique or a genuine attempt to move a company towards a more responsible operating position. More recently, the term social business has joined the lexicon of terms to denote another type of social mission enterprise.

In 2021, the global situation of financial inequality, social malaise, and environmental degradation, has become so severe that what previously seemed too bold now seems imperative, and perhaps not even enough.

Where are the Social Enterprises?

In the UK, there is no agreed Social Enterprise definition, even by Social Enterprise UK the national support agency, therefore it is impossible to know precisely about them. There are, of course, Social Enterprise organisations that have memberships with information about location and type, etc., but this should be used conditionally. Social Enterprise UK estimated that in 2019, there were 80,000 Social Enterprises in the UK; furthermore, they estimated Social Enterprises contributed £24 billion to the economy, and employed nearly a million people. However, Social Enterprise UK's definition is quite broad, and they put forward the following list of criteria:

- Have a clear social and/or environmental mission set out in their governing documents

- Generate the majority of their income through trade
- Reinvest the majority of their profits
- Are autonomous of the State
- Are majority controlled in the interests of the social mission
- Are accountable and transparent

Social Enterprise UK appears to be pointing in the right direction, but the timid nature of the criteria allows for all sorts of misrepresentations. An important factor is an un-business approach; it reads as if running of the commercial enterprise is secondary to the social mission. Social Enterprise needs to be commercial first and foremost, but framed within the social and environmental missions; if it is not financially viable, it is bust.

Internationally, the picture is similar, although organisations such as the British Council support a wide range of Social Enterprise projects in 27 countries throughout the world. Their definition of Social Enterprise is less well defined:

'Social Enterprises are businesses which trade to address social and environmental problems. They generate income like other businesses but reinvest all or most of their profits into their social mission. They create jobs, reduce inequalities and are accountable for their actions, bringing together the entrepreneurial skills of the private sector and the values of public service.'

From looking at just these two examples, we can see that the language is right; the components are nearly there, and the sentiment is supportive. But, are they definitions? To me, the wording is too vague and unprecise, which means that many types of organisations can call themselves a Social Enterprise because they have some of these definitions' characteristics. Over the years and around the world, Social Enterprise definitions have become a free-for-all. In many countries Social Enterprise development agencies have been established, all tend to use the main idea of business with social and environmental purpose, but there is a tendency to interpret the original organisational concept differently. We see that:

Community Interest Company (CIC) UK Government Companies Act 2004 regulation – suggests that by registering as a CIC, you are a Social Enterprise. CIC status is when a company has an asset lock, which means that in the event of the company closing down, its assets will be transferred to a similar company or a charity, but cannot be distributed to owners. The asset lock is useful for community enterprises where ownership of local assets should stay in the community. But for trading enterprises, this can be a liability when trying to secure finance. Furthermore, any private company or other legally registered organisation can also apply and get CIC status. It does not, in any way, regulate ownership approaches, profit distribution, or social and environmental responsibilities. It is absolutely false of the CIC authorising body to claim that if a company is registered with CIC status, they are a Social Enterprise[3].

Social Enterprise Alliance, USA – Social Enterprises are businesses whose primary purpose is the common good. They use the methods and disciplines of business and the power of the marketplace to advance their social, environmental, and human justice agendas. Furthermore, it states that 'a social enterprise is an organisation or initiative that marries the social mission of a non-profit or government program with the market-driven approach of a business'.

Social Traders, Australia – Social enterprises are businesses that trade to intentionally tackle social problems, improve

---

[3] Office of the Regulator of Community Interest Company UK

communities, provide access for people to employment and training, or help the environment.

The Asian Development Bank's India Social Enterprise Landscape Report – This looks at Social Enterprises in terms of triple bottom line returns. 'They address social and environmental needs, such as affordable health services and energy, and have a financially sustainable revenue model (or plan to become sustainable in the near future).'

Social Enterprise Council of Canada – Social enterprises are community-based businesses that sell goods or services in the market place to achieve a social, cultural, and/or environmental purpose; they reinvest their profits to maximise their social mission.

European Union: the definition of a social enterprise is built along three dimensions – an entrepreneurial dimension (with earned income generated by the sale of goods/services on the market, including through public contracting); a social dimension (the pursuit of an explicit social aim, and delivery of products/ services with a social connotation); a governance dimension (accountability, participation, and transparency).

Intellecap in India – recognises Social Enterprises as independent businesses 'with the goal of generating profit', having an 'explicit mission to create social impact', whose operations 'directly improve the lives and livelihoods of those residing at the bottom of the social pyramid'.

The British Council – Social enterprises are businesses which trade to address social and environmental problems and are 'defined by their impact'. They generate income like other businesses, but reinvest all or most of their profits into their social mission. They create jobs, reduce inequalities, and are accountable for their actions, bringing together the entrepreneurial skills of the private sector and the values of public service.

These definitions from some countries' agencies are mainly focused on the mission and reinvestment. At first glance, these definitions might all seem very similar, but they lack any inclusion and understanding of the structural need for legally binding shared ownership and democratic decision-making. They focus on the mission, not the organisational structure of ownership and control. The common threads that weave throughout the narrative are of social, environmental, fiscal responsibility, and independence. And the word 'mission' is used more than others. These are mission-driven, in the most part, privately owned by one to three directors, not co-operatively organised or having shared ownership in any way. They are private businesses that have adopted quasi 'social missions', often for marketing purposes, and they do not include any reference to accountability for their operations. Quite simply, how do we know if they fulfil their social and environmental purpose?

Many multinational corporations, impact investment finance companies, and a host of international and local governmental public bodies, also apply the same social mission statements in their publicity. It is, of course, excellent to see these organisations start to focus on their external responsibilities, and good to see tripartite criteria, in most cases, leading the mission focus. However, what are the results? Again, there is no form of Social Accounting and Audit or regular reporting on their social and environmental missions' results, creating opportunity for falsification and consequent mistrust.

We see definitions that state their 'impact will define them'. This is of course nonsense; impact (having a positive society-wide influence) is comprised of many inputs from a range of stakeholders, so the idea that you can apportion attribution in any meaningful way is simply unrealistic. What could be said is that 'we intend to have a positive impact through the use of our inputs, activities, outputs, and outcome'. To define Social Enterprise based on impact indicates that some people are just not thinking through the ramifications of such a statement. The impact often takes many years to be realised, and includes contributions from many other stakeholders. In order to measure impact and account for the attribution of an organisation's contribution at that level, requires years of social accounting – gathering, recording, and analysing data for outputs and outcome, as proof of the level of contribution to the final stage of impact. Without the gradual and accumulated accounting, the measurement of impact can be misleading and more expensive than the cost of providing the specific service to achieve the intended result.

My concern here, of course, is not to catch these agencies out, but to prevent the term Social Enterprise from becoming meaningless. It is too easy for an organisation to call itself a Social Enterprise and get the benefit (by this, I mean government support or customer loyalty), but not actually be a Social Enterprise. It would be better to have a proper definition, one that can be verified and is legally defined by law. It would be easy to construct a sliding scale of degrees of types of enterprise that fitted, from a mission-only enterprise to a legally registered Social Enterprise.

After Muhammad Yunus won the Nobel Peace Prize in 2006, he started to use the term Social Business as a way of describing projects for poor people that received technical support from multinational corporations for a given period of time. The aim was that by the end of the support, the project converted to an enterprise as a viable business. In recent times, the term Social Business has replaced the term social entrepreneurship, and been used, intermittently, in the same paragraphs with the term Social Enterprise. This continuing reinvention, unfortunately, caused further confusion. In 2012, the European Commission also started to use the term Social Business. However, by 2016, the European Commission rightly abandoned the term Social Business and replaced it with the term, Social Enterprise and the Social Economy.

Since 2008, the Social Enterprise World Forum has organised international conferences around the world, which continue to attract increasing interest from governments, institutions, and people. There are recent and positive developments in edging towards a definition of Social Enterprise that truly represents an alternative to private ownership and the single bottom line value. The British Council is perhaps the most widely engaged international organisation in supporting Social Enterprise in the world; it launched the Social Entrepreneurship Programme in 2009, which is now, in 2021, called the Global Social Enterprise Programme. The European Commission focuses on job creation, and uses any legitimate model to achieve this aim. It established a working group on Social Enterprise, called Expert Group on Social Entrepreneurship (2011-2018), and set up the Social Business Initiative (SBI) in 2011. After spending eight years preparing papers, they decided to change the name of the group to the Expert Group on Social Economy and Social Enterprises (GECES) (2018-2024). Both these influential organisations have now realigned to more clearly focus on Social Enterprise. It was unfortunate that it took so long to discover what was already well known: that muddling terms and definitions only thwarts progress in developing social economy enterprise and jobs. Social Enterprise is also embedded within more extensive programmes, such as the UN's Economic and Social Commission for Asia and the Pacific (ESCAP), where the 17 Sustainable Development Goals (SDG) govern their work, and they partner organisations such as the British Council.

During the 42 years since Social Enterprise first emerged, many countries have attempted to reconcile their mode of social ventures with some notion of Social Enterprise. Social Enterprise is not a movement against anything; it is a movement for constructive change in the values used for running organisations, and the financial, social, and environmental benefits accruing to local economies and communities. It is supported by governments and finance agencies, and finds expression in all sorts of organisations, from community enterprise to wildlife habitat biosphere reserves, and from industrial and innovative industries to health and social care companies. But due to the lack of clear and agreed definitions, these initiatives are mostly self-learning, groups having to learn en route what a Social Enterprise is and how it works.

Sometimes, people express the sentiment that it doesn't matter how these enterprises are formed, but only that they create a positive impact socially and environmentally. I am suspicious of this approach, because how an enterprise is structured, owned, and managed is all about the long-term and sustainable impact. In contrast, the mission-only enterprises rely on the goodwill of owners and controllers that over time wears thin. Social Enterprise cuts across cultures, language, historical backgrounds, and natural habitats; it is universal in its application, because it is fundamentally about what matters to people. Importantly, if Social Enterprise is to survive and prosper as an up-to-date and beneficial organisational structure, I believe it is essential to agree on a precise definition to make progress beyond the rhetorical outbursts from politicians and financial investors. It is time to be truly international in defining Social Enterprise standards and values, to establish a genuine alternative to cater for today's needs.

3 THE EVOLUTION OF SOCIAL ENTERPRISE

The origins of Social Enterprise and cooperative forms of organisation can be traced to the early social struggles of the 17th century, at the very end of the English Civil War. In the UK, a group called 'the Diggers' took over land and cultivated it in common, organised themselves around the idea of one person one vote, and the equal distribution of wealth. This first experiment in cooperative forms of organisation established the idea of integrating social and commercial activities. What the Diggers lacked was ownership of the land they had taken over, and thus they were eventually driven off, and dispersed.

Much later on, other cooperative forms of organisation began to appear. In 1830, several unemployed millers took over the operation of an old unused mill in Hull, to provide flour for their families and other members of the community who were in need. As with the Diggers two centuries earlier, their aims were more social than profit-orientated, and like the Diggers, they did not own the mill and were finally moved out.

As private ownership in business gained ascendancy, pioneers such as Robert Owen (1771-1858) urged the working classes to set up groups of producers with common ownership of the means of production. He advocated the idea of cooperatives not solely for commercial purposes, but in the areas of health and education, and integrating community and commercial values. Owen's ideas were extremely popular. As a result, many cooperative societies and shops were founded, 'Labour exchanges' were set up, and the concept of alternative business models were developed.

The Rochdale Society of Equitable Pioneers (1844), the first manifestation of the Co-op, extended their influence beyond the immediate consumer to the broader interests of the community. Ideas of democratic management and voting rights were part of their doctrine. In Yorkshire, the county where Rochdale is situated, volunteers, literally, ran from village to village explaining what a cooperative was and inspiring local people to set up and form cooperative societies. Many are still operating to this day.

Many of the areas of the welfare state in the UK today owe their origin to the Cooperative Societies. They used their resources to promote free education for all primary-aged children and provide free medical care for workers and their families. Also, the Societies used their meeting halls to run adult education. The first major principle of the traditional cooperative movement was open membership to all on a voluntary basis. Members are entitled to a dividend as a percentage of the amount they spend. The Cooperative Societies had shops and other provisions in every small town and large city. Since the mid-19th century, cooperative societies in the UK pioneered the supermarket, the 'cradle to grave' strapline offering baby food and nursery provision, finance, household goods, food, and funeral services. In its heyday, the Cooperative was the biggest chain of shops in the UK. Over time, however, this created, in the UK, a large, unwieldy consumer membership which lost sight of its core principles. In Europe too, agricultural and financial credit cooperatives were formed, and to this day still make up a sizable commercial sector.

Agricultural purchasing and marketing cooperatives became popular in many developing countries in Asia, South Pacific, and Africa, but over time the State took over their ownership and running, and many cooperatives became uncompetitive and ceased trading; some were annexed as part of the State's instrument for organising small producers and exporting cash crops, such as coffee and cocoa. Because the State ran these cooperatives, exported their crops, and received foreign exchange income, payment to farmers and suppliers lagged far behind delivery dates. Eventually, the farmers, who were the members, started to bypass the cooperatives and deal directly with private traders who, although charging a higher fee, at least paid on time.

In Europe, there are some impressive common ownership enterprises, such as the John Lewis Partnership in the UK – established in 1929, with a current turnover in 2019 of £10.2 billion, and employing 83,000 workers/partners. In Spain, the Mondragon Corporation – a federation of worker cooperatives, based in the Basque region, was founded in 1956 by graduates of a local technical college. It now has an annual turnover of €12 billion, and employs 74,000 employees/members. But the largest concentration of employee-owned enterprises is in Italy, with over 800,000 people engaged in worker cooperatives and social co-ops. Unlike other European countries, Italian cooperatives benefit from tax advantages, due to their perceived social benefits. Article 45 of the Italian Constitution states that 'the Republic recognises the social function of co-operation with mutual character and without private speculation purposes'. Profits in Italian co-ops are exempt from tax, as long as they are re-invested in the cooperative. The requirement under the current Italian law is that at least 30% of the annual net profit must be allocated to an indivisible reserve. The State law promotes and favours its growth with the most appropriate means, and ensures, with appropriate controls, its character and purposes.

In the 20th century, cooperative enterprises based on collective forms of ownership by the workforces emerged in the UK and other European countries. These were known as workers cooperatives, and were joined by employee ownership companies under the auspice of ICOM (the Industrial Common Ownership Movement) which, in 1976, successfully promoted the Industrial Common Ownership Act in the UK Parliament. This Act recognised common ownership model rules, which were to play an important part in developing worker cooperatives in the UK.

What had gone wrong in the traditional co-op movement was, to my thinking, that there had been no attempt to measure social goals, which as a result became less visible. This led eventually to a situation where employees and customers were members of the consumer cooperatives but had little or no idea what they were or stood for. This was a major spur for the development of the Social Accounting and Audit ideas put forward at that time. Although cooperatives and employee-owned enterprises had both commercial and social objectives, they only accounted for the commercial operations. They left out the social mission as extra-commercial – treating it as an externality, and not an integral part of the organisation.

In 1978, at Beechwood College in Leeds, UK, the concept and structure of Social Enterprise was firmly established and defined. Social Enterprise had the basic rules of workers cooperatives and common ownership businesses, with each worker/member (co-owner)[4] owning one share, and each share giving that member one vote in the general governance of the enterprise. In addition to the importance of cooperative forms of ownership, the social and ecological missions were added, whereby the enterprise took on responsibility for not only being financially viable, but for creating social wealth and being environmentally responsible

---

[4] Membership and co-owning are the same in Social Enterprise, and because the term membership has become associated with the idea of distance and occasional involvement, I have used the term co-owner instead; I hope it denotes a more engaging approach to being a member and, by law, an owner of an organisation.

in the way it operated. The internal Social Accounting and Audit system, developed at that time, integrated the social, environmental, and financial aspects into one management and reporting system.

In the 1990s, the neoliberal economic alliance between Prime Minister Mrs Thatcher in the UK and President Regan in the USA pressured the United Nations to stop support to any venture with the word 'cooperative' in its title. They were both strong supporters and believers in individual entrepreneurship, and loathed the notion of collective action. Mrs Thatcher famously said that 'there is no such thing as society; there are individual men and women'. This viewpoint affected developing countries' ability to raise funds to support cooperatives and create the necessary infrastructure to start new ones or grow existing cooperatives. The vitality of people working together in cooperative ventures was undermined, and unfortunately had long-term negative consequence; even today, many cooperatives in developing countries suffer from government inaction and investor apathy.

Today, in Britain, Social Enterprises are supported by Social Enterprise UK – a national think tank and support agency that works with regional support agencies around the country. Together, they have been responsible for mainstreaming Social Enterprise in the UK and driving the Public Sector Social Value Act 2012 through Parliament. The Social Value Act enables public bodies to use social value as part of their contract award criteria when procuring goods and services from the private sector. The Act calls for all public sectors commissioning to factor in economic, social, and environmental wellbeing.

In the European Union, a similar directive was issued to cover the period 2004/18, which came into force in April

2004, covering public works contracts, public supply contracts, and public service contracts. It directs the Member States to include clauses in their public procurement processes on social and environmental good practice. Research into how different countries in Europe interpreted and used the directive has been undertaken: it shows a mixed response. The one finding most often cited is the lack of clarity and definition of a Social Enterprise. Without an agreed Social Enterprise definition, it has not been possible for public authorities in the European Union to legally contract with Social Enterprise. One finding suggests: 'Due to the informality of the definition of a Social Enterprise, across Member States, public officials are rightly concerned that in issuing tenders and awarding contracts to Social Enterprises they may be challenged by competitors who were unsuccessful on the grounds of bias.' What is needed, the research concludes, is for Social Enterprise to adopt a clear and agreed definition, and formulate legal charters in such a way as to represent that definition, furthermore, to use some form of Social Accounting and Audit to plan, measure, and report on performance to prove that Social Enterprise fulfilled its stated purposes.

3.1 Types of Social Enterprises

Social Enterprise has become an umbrella term to define a range of different types of trading and social provision organisations and companies. In the UK, there are many thousands of Social Enterprises, from large department stores employing tens of thousands of staff, to very small specialist support agencies employing two or three staff. Across the world, in Europe, Asia, Africa, and the Americas, Social Enterprises are starting to emerge as an important microeconomic force.

In each country, the regulatory frameworks are different, and determine the type of legal structure Social Enterprises can use.

Most business regulatory systems use charters (constitutions) to describe and register a business. This automatically means that the business has limited liability, and the individual members are not liable for any debts. The same is the case for Social Enterprise, but because there are no specific charters designed for them, each group has to adapt inappropriate constitutions by designing appropriate clauses and adding new ones. For example, it is possible to use a joint-stock company charter (a traditional private sector business model) by writing in the charter specifically who can be shareholders. Such as, only paid staff, or residents in a defined geographical community, and limiting their share value to a nominal value so that all net profits are re-invested. Thus creating the basic defining elements of a Social Enterprise from a traditional business model. In addition, in many countries, there are already existing forms for associations and cooperatives that are legally registered and can trade.

The UK regulatory options include Company Limited by Guarantee; Industrial and Provident Societies; Charitable Status; Incorporated Associations; and Joint Stock Company limited by equal shareholding. They can trade in any commercial sector and/or support any social or environmental endeavour, but in some countries, due to their legal structures and Acts of Government, they are sometimes restricted to particular sectors or limited in their trading partners. Within this overall context, there are four main sectors in which Social Enterprise is applicable.

Commercial Trading – buying and selling goods and services in all sectors, including agriculture, manufacturing, IT, retail, transport, and warehousing; there is no sector inaccessible to Social Enterprise. There are employee-owned enterprises: sometimes these have traditional management hierarchies and salary levels, but with less severe differentials, or they may be small worker cooperatives with only a few directors/employees who work in less hierarchical ways and practice wage parity. The common characteristic is that workers are the owners and govern the company democratically, and include social and environmental responsibility for their operation.

Financial Services – such as Savings and Loans organisations, like credit unions, microcredit organisations, cooperative banks, and membership-based revolving loan funds. Credit Unions were first established in the 1850s in Germany, and spread internationally. Cooperative Banks have likewise been around since the 1870s, owned as a subsidiary of a membership cooperative. In recent times, microcredit organisations have sprung up in many developing countries to great effect, after the success of the Grameen Bank in Bangladesh. Social Impact Stock Exchanges are emerging in Europe and Asia, and Social Enterprise is eligible to tap into these to raise finance.

Community Organisations – many community organisations are registered Social Enterprises. This includes community enterprises, housing cooperatives, community interest companies with asset locks, community centres, pubs, and shops, associations, housing associations, and football clubs. These are membership organisations that usually exist for a specific purpose, and trade commercially. All operate to re-invest profits into the organisation and the community. They have large memberships who are customers or supporters of the organisation's key purpose. There are examples of village cooperatives in Pakistan, India, and Bangladesh, that were established as far back as 1904. In the UK, there are many multifunctional community-based organisations with a geographical membership of residents, usually holding assets such as buildings, land, tools, and machinery, which are used to provide social care support to residents and as assets against which finance can be leveraged.

The term Community Enterprise was coined in the 1980s at Beechwood College, to distinguish the Social Enterprise-style community organisation from those that did not include the triple bottom line. Community Enterprises are multifunctional, membership-owned, profit and non-profit organisations. They are owned and controlled by members who are either based in a geographical area like a village or a housing estate, or who share a common interest such as campaigning groups or specialists developing good practices. Community enterprises own assets such as property, land, tools, and machinery. They provide local support for new ventures, manage commercial trading enterprises, and non-trading community social provision. They are legally registered and have limited liability, and practise asset locks over their assets. This means they can only sell assets if the income received is used for community purposes or donated to similar organisations.

Trading Subsidiaries – there are many Civil Society Organisations and charities that operate a commercial consultancy and training enterprise, or subsidiary trading enterprises, such as Oxfam in the UK that owns and runs many high street shops selling second-hand clothes and household items. The profits are used to provide salaries for people who offer free services to specific groups of people, or to further the social or environmental aims of the host organisation. The charity or community sector organisations acts as a holding company, owning trading enterprises and receiving the profits/surpluses that is re-invested into the community – in some countries, tax-free.

As Yuval Harari pointed out in his seminal work[5], one of the most profound characteristics of homo sapiens is their ability

---

[5] *Sapiens - A Brief History of Humankind*, Yuval Noah Harari, 2014

and capacity to organise themselves. With our evolutionary history behind us, people are capable of organising themselves in myriad configurations and organisational structures, and can enter into any commercial and non-commercial sector. Social Enterprise is more versatile than other structures: it can be commercial, focusing on buying and selling goods and services; non-profit making, as a charitable organisation; purely social, in the form of a non-trading community organisation; or it can be an environmental group, owning and managing biodiversity nature reserves.

The mistake often made is to involve lawyers in the design of the Social Enterprise organisational charter. It is right that they should vet and help formulate a charter, but they should not design one. Lawyers hold high authority, and many people lack the confidence to debate and challenge what they say. They too often don't understand what the Social Enterprise wants, and just advise the same approach as to a small business, or they lack the confidence to submit new ideas when registering a Social Enterprise. From my experience, the best way is for members of the Social Enterprise to design their system according to how they wish to operate, and use the outline as the specifications for lawyers to construct a legal charter around. Lawyers, like most professionals, need to be instructed by their clients before designing charters, and need to be encouraged to be bold when submitting new forms of legal charters to registering bodies.

4 VALUES TO DRIVE OBJECTIVES AND ACTIONS

Values are the basis on which people set their priorities and determine right from wrong. They underpin society and the individual. Different people can see the same thing at the same time and in the same place, but each person's values determine how they perceive and respond to what they see and experience. Because values are learned or created, they can be changed; they are not static, but dynamic, and need to evolve to keep up with new experiences.

Social Enterprise brings together a set of values to establish new and updated ways of working and to provide operational guidance in decision-making. In Social Enterprise, we combine common ownership, democracy, financial viability, social wealth creation, and environmental responsibility into one set of values that, put together, can lead to a change of behaviour. The values are not new in themselves; their combination leads to the newness and vitality.

Objectives and activities are the specific things individuals and groups use to plan and implement values. Objectives reflect a particular value or values and will be measured against these, as well as specific planned targets. The coherence between values and objectives are at the heart of Social Enterprise. Do the means (objectives and actions) justify the ends (impact and values)?

Means to end

The means to end dichotomy has been used to justify bad behaviour; for example, the value of profit maximisation is often at the expense of environmental degradation. The excuse that the end justifies the means no longer holds, if it ever did. We can control the means (resources, preparations, activities, and outputs) but not the end (the impact and benefit to society). The end is subject to other stakeholders and a range of variables, circumstances, and assumptions outside of our control. Therefore, if we take care of what we can control, the means, and understand the external influences and assumptions, we have a better chance of reaching an outcome that in the end achieves a successful impact. What's the point, for example, of making loads of money, only to find that the environment in which one had planned to enjoy the benefits was denuded and inhospitable?

Today, the means are becoming more important than the end. To degrade the environment to make a financial profit is no longer acceptable. We must stop the pollution and harmful productive wastes now, not at some point in the distant future. Therefore, the value is less with the end and more with the means; let's bring them together into a new way of thinking and operating, so that over time the means and ends become synonymous with viability and regenerative approaches. As the means is controllable, this is where we should apply the regenerative values to drive objectives and actions.

Sustainability

Sustainability (the ability to be maintained at a given level) has been used, since the Brundtland Report for the World Commission on Environment and Development (1987), as a value term to help plan and measure development programmes that don't damage the environment and that do achieve beneficial outcomes and impact for specific target stakeholders.

'Sustainability' is splashed across the headlines of corporate responsibility reports and corporate advertising; they have recognised the value of sustainability too late. As usual, the corporate world is behind the curve. We know that sustainability is no longer enough; it once was, but it would have meant that the corporate world would have had to adopt sustainability policies and actions much earlier. It is too late because sustaining the present levels of pollution, inequality, false media, etc., is no longer an option; it's already indefensible. For societies in many countries, the level of regressive behaviour has reached such a level that sustainability is useless. By only focusing on sustainability, we have overlooked the damage being wrought in other ways, such as the accumulation of owned assets by a small cohort of people. This must not be allowed to continue; the level of inequality already common in our society cannot be maintained; the level of tolerance by the many is wearing thin, and will continue to boil over on occasions until it turns into an unstoppable explosion. Ownership of huge assets in so few hands is anti-social and dangerous; ownership must become value based. There have to be limits, in a finite world, on how much a single person or State can own. Commonly owned land, water, and air are not technical issues, they are value issues – being the substance of life – and need to be held in trust by and for the benefit of society, not treated like a commodity to be sold and bought.

It is now essential that, going forward, everything from infrastructure to social care needs a regenerative value; goods and services needing in some way to be designed to be renewable. House building should be designed using appropriate materials, and be powered by renewable energy, and all newly manufactured products should be reusable or biodegradable. The argument about GM crops is not about science; it's about the absence of regenerative content, i.e. they don't produce seeds that can be used to grow new plants. This non-regenerative approach permeates much of our society's use of natural and handmade goods. The non-regenerative approach will be seen, in the future, as essentially regressive, anti-social, and anti-human. It is likely to be seen in the same way we today see slavery, asbestos, smoking, and terrorism. One day, we will look back in amazement and horror at the vast waste of natural resources and the pollution we produce, and our grandchildren will say of us – 'how stupid!'

Regenerative values

Regeneration has been with us since the 1930s. After the Great Depression, attempts to redress the imbalance of wealth felt by some communities started to gather momentum. Regeneration is not an end; it is the means to countering the existential ills our global society faces. Unlike direct support, regenerative support has taken on a broader and more inclusive range of factors, such as financial investment in new machinery, skills, health, and education, along with infrastructure and, in the UK, devolving some key government departments to regions of high unemployment. For example, the relocation of the Driver and Vehicle Licensing Agency (DVLA) office to Swansea, the Passport Office to Newport, and Companies House to Cardiff in the 1960s, was an attempt to create renewal in areas where the old mining and steel industries once stood proud.

During the 1980s, we saw large regeneration programmes in areas such as the Docklands in Liverpool, London, and in regional centres. Perhaps one of the most ambitious and radical was the 1990s New Deal for Communities regeneration programme, with an overall budget of £2 billion. These have shaped our understanding of regeneration. Yet our approach now needs to be very different from these short-term isolated interventions. The role of regenerative approaches has to become integral to most of what we do, and be woven into the fabric of manufacturing, infrastructure, and organisational behaviour. If the government imposed fiscal measures on non-regenerative products at the same rate as they do for tax on cigarettes, manufacturers would soon change the designs and the materials they use. For example, there is no excuse in 2021 not to insist that every new building – houses, factories, offices, service properties – be designed as passive buildings, with water catchment systems and integral south-facing roofs made with photovoltaic materials. Not only would the building use fewer natural resources, be financially cheaper, and create zero emissions, but importantly we would feel more intelligent and good about our governance. Furthermore, it is high time to put regenerative values at the heart of our technical and management educational system.

Impact

At some level, to know how an initiative impacts on society is essential when designing and implementing new developments. However, with the emphasis on 'impact investment' or 'social impact investing', we see the ends and means dichotomy widen. The impact is beyond the outcome and always relies on other inputs from other stakeholders and, often, society itself. The outcome is when an initiative is realised, i.e. we put in a water facility for a village, and the outcome is clean water and healthy people. The impact of that initiative is that these healthy people can go to work and earn more money, attend school, and get better educated, and generally spend more time being healthy and enjoying life. But the impact is dependent on a range of variables and assumptions, and can take years to be fully realised. In the meantime, while trying to achieve the end impact, we suffer because the method of developing the impact may be detrimental to those involved, the means. For example, I witnessed communities' land being commandeered to provide space for planting eucalyptus trees for long term growth and export and they were left with less cultivatable land in the short to medium term. Impact is beyond our control, and we should be very mindful of recognising our inability to understand and plan for impact adequately. The recent fashion with impact investment if not carefully thought through can be likened to escapism: 'don't worry about anything and just do the same, but with a long-term aim of doing good in the future.'

Impact can often be unintentional, and can be either positive or negative. By the time an outcome or initiative is realised, and before impact is being experienced, circumstances can and often have changed, and the desired benefits will be compromised by unforeseen events or unrealised assumptions. For example, a water well building programme I was involved with in Bangladesh, providing clean water, worked for about 30 years in certain coastal areas of the country. Then, due to overuse and rising sea levels, the impact they achieved was reversed, and the villages are now drawing saltwater from their wells and becoming sick again. In development, the unintentional impact is all too common. Because we are dealing with technical, social, and environmental influences, the complexity in achieving a stated impact is always problematic, and therefore often unreliable as the end goal. Unless planning for impact is very detailed, with analysed assumptions linked to risk mitigation assessments, the intentional impact can be simply a justification for any investment and activity. After 40 years of working in impact planning, my experience is that while impact most definitely happens, it takes time, and when you get there it's often not quite what was expected. Achieving it can be like chasing the pot of gold; it just might be there, if only we could find the rainbow's end.

Combined values – the whole worth

Today, with such extreme threats to existence, we need sustainability plus and we need to start thinking in terms of regenerative progression; less about more stuff, and more about less stuff, but with higher output value and longer life expectancy. This must begin at the design and fabrication. Everything must last, with the brief to be reusable, and then engineered for that result. It is necessary to create new hybrid values that fuse the means to ends with viability and sustainability to be regenerative. New values come from unrestricted environments where individuals and groups are free to dream up new ways of seeing what has always been seen, but from another standpoint and new point of view.

In the 1970s, we had moved beyond the Western teenagers' rebellion against the old social and family hierarchies, and embraced new fashion, music, diets, relationships, attitudes to armaments, and open thinking. It was a tremendous time for innovation; old ideas were updated and reaffirmed, and society was open to completely new ideas. That thinking was less of theoretical ideas and philosophical concepts, and more of practical action. We just did things, and while this was right and exciting and innovative, it left out the vital part of the equation – the values to support the actions; these were, by and large, absent.

During this time, these initiatives were practising a circular regenerative economy, one that designed out waste and pollution and built in reuse and recycling wherever possible, without the theoretical context and terms. Not only were these new values about opposing war or corporate greed, they were also affirmative, supporting renewable energy technologies, community forms of living, feminism, organic cultivation, and many other, now 'mainstream', ideas. The new values and fashions ushered in alternatives to corporate convention, but they were weak and unorganised; the corporate profit value won out, and global neoliberalism was born. It is much more comfortable and profitable to introduce new technologies like computers and the mobile phone that disrupt existing goods and services. Those across the political spectrum supported these technological ideas and gadgets which make money, rather than societal and behaviour change. Ideas such as organic cultivation and renewable energy generation, that were seen to be either unprofitable or that might challenge the profitability for existing corporations, were seen as 'left-wing'. Unfortunately, making money was, and is still, seen as of higher value than, say, saving the planet.

For people like me, making money was less important than saving the planet, building local wealth, or being equal with women. So, while living at Lifespan commune in South Yorkshire in the early 1970s, I heeded Marx's advice to split the day into three: physical work, mental work, and play. I started to spend time not just doing physical work, but also spending some time thinking. Lifespan was all about the practical and the physical: just do it, and stop talking so much. But when you looked around Lifespan, it was bursting at the seams with new values. We educated our children; women and men shared equal status; shared resources, decision-making was democratic; we built renewable energy machines; cultivated the land organically; recycled waste; and we were more in favour of doing these things than we were against things we didn't like. Lifespan was a positive and affirmative collection of practical actions. Yet without any coherent philosophical underpinning of values, it became too dependent on the current view and fad of the present individuals, and lacked wider appeal. Why didn't we get across what we understood about plastic bags, for example? We knew they were environmentally damaging in the early 1970s, but we lacked the conceptual framework and values to support the message and tell the story.

At Lifespan, 'sustainability' was not adequate to describe how we worked and lived. We weren't sustaining anything. We were creating regenerative new things and new ways of behaving. We were regenerating our environment, our economy, and our community. We had gone beyond the point of sustainability, we were in a position where we needed to heal the social inequality, the environmental degradation, and the financial poverty – and the only way we found to regenerate these was setting up an alternative set of tripartite values.

Financial, social, and environmental values are more complex than a profit and loss bottom line, and are prone to a wider range of variables and mood changes than only being focused on financial gain. When you squeeze multiple values into narrow indicators, too much is left out, or even worse, results are skewed to give incorrect data. Values need to focus not on the financial profit or loss result or the investment targets, so much as the way the results are achieved, and the means used. The value has to contain the means as much as the end; it is time to integrate them into one process. Profit and loss are such simple, independent, and inconsiderate values that they have now become dangerous and irresponsible. It is time to ban the practice of the single bottom line as the method for measuring commercial organisations' operational performance. It is time to move towards joined-up values that reflect our current joined-up physical, social, emotional, and environmental realities.

Social Enterprise from its beginning has been about values, replacing one set of values with another set of values; about creative destruction. That is why Social Accounting and Audit was originally presented as a non-compulsory monitoring process. The idea was to enable groups to experiment and test new values and measurement methods in their structures and decision-making methods. To facilitate change towards regenerative and restorative models of organisation and economy.

Creating values

Social Accounting and Audit was the first internal organisational approach to providing a structured way of developing commercial enterprises that supported the new set of tripartite values. Within this context, the new values provide a framework to plan, implement, and measure performance. By integrating the tripartite values into one system, organisations can start to use the values to help change direction and behaviour to achieve a more rounded approach to good practice.

Changing values takes time; the process has to grapple with an array of internal and external influences that are either supportive or hostile. The Social Accounting and Audit system supports the transition to engage with workers and customers, moving from a single financial value to a triple set of values. The customer base provides the external influences and pressures on the Social Enterprise to organise and apply the triple values and report on their performance. The internal system is participative, and the external pressure is coercive; together they form the perfect conditions for change.

Participative change starts with knowledge of the problem that needs changing. This knowledge, if open and discussed, leads to a shift in attitude. Some individuals will change more quickly than others, leading to behavioural change. Once a critical mass of individual behaviour has been reached, the enterprise enacts organisational behavioural change that then needs to be consolidated into new management rules and systems. This is not linear, but iterative and circular, and through trial and error, change comes to pass. Coercive change starts with rules and laws, and once a critical mass of feeling is expressed, the pressure to change is motivated externally and enforceable.

For example, during the 1980/90s, smoking became recognised as a major cause of cancer and governments around the world invested in trying to reduce its use. How we stopped smoking: as a trainer during this period, each course would start with a discussion about whether or not this was a no smoking venue. This discussion sometimes decided one way or the other, or half the room was for smokers, and the other half for non-smokers. The debate was always tetchy, sometimes resulting in participants storming out of the place not to return; other times it was amicable, and certain people would give way. But it was always a pain. Over time, the shifts from the majority of participants being smokers to non-smokers grew, as more people learned about the danger and cost of smoking. Eventually, the coercive element settled the matter, and smoking was banned in the room and building. At this point, it ceased being an issue, but it did need both the participation and discussion to learn, and the coercive ban to cement the change. In recent time, trainers will have experienced the same with the issue of mobile phones.

An example of reinforcing behaviour is when we have the value of participation combined with the system of democratic decision-making means that a single decision will have created a conclusion and a sense of empowerment through involvement and achieving a result. In my experience, a key reason many capacity-building projects fail is that the intention of empowerment is not supported by the hierarchical organisational system and decision-making methods used to manage and implement the initiative. The means doesn't translate into the end. Empowerment doesn't come about because someone has said the word; it must be experienced by those who are meant to be empowered; the internal coherence is missing. With Social Enterprise, alignment between ownership, democracy, and interest in one of the other values, combines to create internal coherence and, in turn, empowerment. The internal integration is robust and combines to form a long-term regenerative system – it enables individuals to align with their principles in a practical way, and thus experience happiness and fulfilment. The combined mix of principles and policies moves towards a new interpretation of what business is for, and how it should be owned, governed, and be accountable.

Creating values is empowering and enhances ownership

Setting values is one of the most effective tools for empowerment and capacity building. Values enable individuals and groups to set their agenda and standards, and allow groups to learn the confidence and ability to take responsibility for their personal and organisational affairs. Discussing principles and policies is a valuable learning experience for any group of people. This is partly because the group has moved back from practical decision-making, and as the debate tends to be wide-ranging, intellectual, and relaxing, with no pressure to make decisions, it enables groups to explore each other's views in an emotionally safe way.

The framework for the Social Accounting and Audit system uses a hierarchy of inputs at the bottom, leading to activities, outputs, and outcomes, which then impact in the broader society. This framework is used to plan, manage, and measure organisational performance. This approach integrates the six Social Enterprise values, creating consistency between the means and the end into a single method where people have both the control and responsibility for their actions, and where they can be held accountable for their organisational behaviour.

When an organisation moves from a single bottom line to multiple bottom lines, to a rounded planning and measuring approach, it does not mean that it takes the three components of social, financial, and environmental as parallel plans and audits. No, it moves beyond the three and combines them into one, a hybrid of the three – the whole is greater than the sum of its parts. The combination can be singular in practice. We might plan the development of a physical product and, attached to that plan, an assessment of the social, financial, and environmental influences, along with more traditional concerns about markets, machinery, skills, investment, etc. This approach will become second nature after a short while, and not only prevent poor decision-making but is likely to improve the quality of the product and its long-term regenerative performance.

Organisational decisions are always supported by values, and the actions that follow should inherently reflect the importance of the value. When there are multiple values, as in Social Enterprise, vertical coherence between meaning and action must be complemented with lateral coherence between other, equally important, values and their associated actions. The mix of multiple values and the many interdependent associated actions will, I would argue, generate new insights, helping improve organisational performance for the benefit of achieving the triple bottom line objectives and impacts.

5 SOLUTIONS TO OUR PROBLEMS

The world's problems are multiple and multifaceted. For the many, it is a case of not being able to afford and satisfy basic physiological needs; others are caught by politically false information and left feeling confused and unsafe; some are isolated and lonely in a sea of social media, or trapped in the structural web of corporate control and personal irrelevance. The planet is experiencing bushfires, droughts, floods, cyclones, pandemics, and sea level rises that are becoming more severe year by year, and still we behave as though this is normal. It is not normal, and it looks as though it is getting worse – to the extent that for many people, Maslow's hierarchy of needs[6] is becoming an inverted hierarchy of despair. With a hierarchy of despair, Maslow's idea of how people are motivated loses momentum, and the building blocks to the good life crumble away.

A civil society with facilities free at the point of use has been replaced by corporate structures that charge for everything at the point of use; you can't even have a pee unless you've got the money. Society is about people living together, sharing resources and facilities for the benefit of the group. But galloping corporate greed has shattered the notion of civil society, replacing it with a creed of 'you get what you pay for', and if you haven't got any

---

[6] Maslow's theory was fully expressed in his 1954 book *Motivation and Personality*. Maslow's hierarchy of needs is a motivational theory in psychology, comprising a five-tier model of human needs, often depicted as hierarchical levels within a pyramid. From the bottom of the hierarchy upwards, the needs are: physiological (food and clothing), safety (job security), love and belonging needs (friendship), esteem, and self-actualization.

money… well, you get nothing. The rage on the streets is a cry for the re-emergence of civil society around the world, a society that has care and kindness not greed and exploitation at its core.

All the soothing words from politicians won't alter the fact that the problems we face are structural, and need structural change. We see it expressed on the streets in Hong Kong, Paris, Sudan, Russia, and Argentina, and many more places. Unremitting migration from the poor south to the prosperous north, and from the vulnerable lands to more secure areas, is only just beginning. It may go in cycles, go up and down, or may be triggered by explosive events, but what is sure is that migration won't lessen until civil society functions as a common resource for all.

So, what are the problems? Is it overpopulation, monopolistic capitalism, social media, environmental degradation, inequality, outdated morality and ethics, obsolete laws, religious beliefs, or technical complexity? Or is it merely that globalisation and giantism have overtaken our governance systems? Have we overwhelmed ourselves and our capacity to govern ourselves? However, and for whatever reason, street protest or illicit border crossings rapidly escalate from single issue to multiple issues, and the initial cause becomes lost in a fog of explosive anger. When we reach endemic prolonged public rage, we as a society are in trouble and cannot ignore the causes. It's not that we don't know what the reason is; we do. It is inequality in all sense of the word. As Yuval Noah Harari says, 'people are feeling irrelevant.'[7]

Is the uncertain future we face an existential threat or a bright new fourth industrial revolution? The answer to this question depends on your level of wealth, where you live, and your mobility. We are in the process of moving from the Holocene

---

[7] Yuval Noah Harari – *Sapiens: A Brief History of Humankind*

epoch, when biology and geology dictated our lifestyle, to the Anthropocene, when humans dictate our lifestyle. The process is happening without us being consciously involved. Evolution has created a species of homo sapiens that has the capacity for thought, can easily communicate, is gregarious, and dexterous. Beyond that, we are now creating artificial homo sapiens that can do everything humans can do, but more predictably and efficiently. But before the world becomes wholly predictable and machines direct us towards the best option, we need to wrest back control. What makes us human is that we are not at all times predictable, and that we are not always efficient; we are fallible.

The Anthropocene epoch is considered the period during which human activity has been the dominant influence on climate, the environment, and geology. It is the age of humans being responsible for the technology and science we create, and the society we vote for, and the environment in which we live. However, the concentration of ownership, power, and influence into ever smaller cohorts of certain people, disempowers wider society from exercising responsibility for the impact they impose. The corporate structure precludes the very essence of the need for more people to take more responsibility for their behaviour and how they interact with society and the planet. The question is: how can people be responsible for their lives if they (we) have no say over what is done?

The economy, like new technology, is running away from our ability to understand and control it. Both are monopolised by small cohorts of people, private asset owners, elected and unelected legislators, and entrepreneurs, who are trying to influence other people's lives disproportionately. In the next 20 years, we are likely to see economics and technology decouple from people. They will both be increasingly independent of the mass of people, and while they are meant to serve us, they are likely to discover they can function much better if we're not around. It's not a matter of humans becoming superfluous; it is more that humans will be seen to be an obstruction to private asset owners' coded missions. The economy always wants to know how to predict the future, and technology still intends to be ultra-efficient. These contradict human needs of being free from predictability, and being outsmarted at every turn by machines. The philosophical idea that human actions are entirely predictable and that machines are so much smarter – for example, AI – raises the profound question: why do we exist? Social media, with its altered reality, may be responsible for why society is in the grip of a state of 'mass psychology of anxiety'. What else explains the situation we are in?

What is upon us is the combination of information technology, biological technology, and artificial intelligence run as big data systems. Together, they either offer huge potential in human health, living conditions, and the biosphere, or by taking over the major functions of work, innovation, management, and decision-making to such an extent of making human beings irrelevant. It depends on who owns and controls the technologies. And at the moment, the very few significant financial shareholders and their CEOs control those technologies, not society. Having ownership of the pervasive technology of AI in the hands of a few unelected people sounds dangerous.

We should also look with concern upon our institutional frameworks; they are not an existential threat, but a societal threat. Societal threats are less about our existence than about how that existence is lived, but as pointed out above, how we work and live needs to change to meet the Anthropocene age. Societal threats are those we experience as exploitation, at the hands of modern capitalism expressed as the 'gig economy', where organised labour has been replaced with individual workers, and organised capital has triumphed. The combined overpopulation of the planet and exploitation of the natural world is now so extreme that only extreme measures will rectify the imbalance and enable humans to take responsibility for the Anthropocene epoch. The loss of historical roots, fragmented communities, no shared experiences, and the inability to mobilise ourselves to deal with threats, has crippled society and made us all individually vulnerable. In this scenario, we are essential, but only so far as we are fodder for the corporations to exploit in the way most people are employed and consume goods and services.

By and large, this is not a fault of something or someone; it is a consequence of our collective action. We did it to ourselves, thinking that growth was the way to go. Now we realise it has gone too far, and so we must stop and re-group civil society at the expense of corporate mission. We have to take a lot more responsibility for our actions on the planet and between ourselves. If we are undertaking such an enormous shift in our relationship with the physical world − our life support system − and by implication, the solar system, should we not be asking ourselves if we want to continue organising as though we are held hostage to the geology and natural environment by the increasing extreme weather pattens we have no control over? Or, do we accept the need to reorganise our way of living and working to reduce the negative impacts on climate and biodiversity and financial and social inequality as much as possible, to control our interaction with the physical and social world in ways which exploit human ingenuity and technology for the benefit of society?

There are six non-exclusive critical areas of threat faced by the majority of people on the planet today. If we invert their negative influences, and turn them into objectives and positive values − these six values underpin Social Enterprise to counter six of the most pressing problems facing the world population.

Problem 1 Structural inequality

Structural inequality is as old as society. For example, the chief (lord, queen, etc., insert as appropriate) has more power than others, and systems such as the Indian caste system still flourish. Once the asset value of owned land, property, and intellectual rights passes a certain point, ordinary people can't enter into owning assets. Common land is usurped by the State and sold for development, and it's gone for eternity. In a global society, ownership, decision-making, influence, and benefit, are tied tightly together into an impenetrable web of power relations and privilege. Structural privilege is something we either benefit from or are disadvantaged by; it's not new, and in small doses can have a marginal impact. But, since the 1970s, the global economy has built up excessive structural inequality. In 2016[8], over 50% of global asset ownership was held by only 1% of the population, with the bottom 71% of the world's population controlling just 3% of the globe's wealth. In 2021, the Chicago Booth Review noted that in America, the 1% can be divided into four categories. The top 0.01% share of wealth accumulated by 20 individuals is now greater than the total wealth of all the other members of the 1% club. As Thomas Piketty[9] found, the rate of return on capital has outpaced the rate of economic growth. When that happens over an extended period of time, the wealthy can see their riches accumulate, while inequality grows worse. Its effect has now reached intolerable levels. It is stifling society, skewing the economy away from its core tenets of open and free trade, and creating a state of irrelevance for billions of people.

---

[8] Oxfam Report, 2016
[9] Thomas Piketty, the author of *Capital in the Twenty-First Century*

Solution 1   Structural equality through Common Ownership

The solution to structural inequality is to share the real and lasting wealth in society, and to own in common physical and intellectual assets. Common Ownership is a pillar guaranteeing human rights – there are legal, social, and financial mechanisms that exist to arrest the decline in commonly owned and shared assets. Social Enterprise is based on common ownership of the enterprise by the people who engage in creating its collective wealth; it is equitable and satisfying, leading to responsible ownership and control. All it needs is the will of people to come together and take responsibility for asset ownership. To own and to control assets is fundamental to reversing the march of the 1% owning everything.

Problem 2   Disenfranchisement

In having no say over what affects us, we lose ownership over assets and shared facilities, and we also lose control of how and what they are used for and managed. Having no voice is the experience for billions of people, and the trend is for fewer people to have a voice, and even fewer people to have a huge voice. If you sit back for a moment and ask if that sounds like a good idea, most people will, I'm sure, say no for two reasons: one is the likelihood of bad decision-making by a very few people who have powerful vested interests in the outcomes that favour them; and secondly, the frustration felt by a large majority of people will lead to outbursts of rage and rebellion. Neither of these options is desirable.

'But we have democracy' is a default response to complaints of disenfranchisement. True, we do have democracy in many countries, and definitely in Europe. However, that democracy is limited in our international relations and our local authorities. It's constrained by corporate plans and the dash for privatisation, and is overridden by false claims and supposedly imperative 'bigger plans'. What elected representatives say during electioneering is often reneged on while in office, with little accountability or redress – not necessarily because they want to, but because they find they have no choice; the vested interests of corporate plans override their civic agendas.

One percent of the world's population own and control over 50% of the world's assets and resources. They control too much in their interests, without a thought for other people. We all make decisions in our own interest, but because the 99% of us own and control fewer assets, our decisions affect very few other people. The 1% has an enormous impact on billions of people. We are all equally fallible, and are prone to making stupid decisions based on some personal experience, a particular bias, or some emotional quirk. In a crowded and technically complex world, can we afford the whims of a single pharaoh or a queen to dictate the way we deal with climate change or homelessness? In a rational society, decisions over the use of huge assets would be curtailed, and made subject to technical, human, and environmental considerations.

Solution 2   Democratic governance

Democracy is the operation of human rights – the solution to the sense of profound disenfranchisement is to share control of the working environment, making sure that structural ownership reflects individuals' rights. Social Enterprise brings control into the hands of those who produce the wealth, and localises active suffrage to all those immediately involved with the process of decision-making and the consequences of those decisions. This will create what Wilhelm Reich called 'work democracy'[10] that governs the organic process of human behaviour through the

---

[10]   Wilhelm Reich, *The Mass Psychology of Fascism*

natural and practical functions of life – love, work, and knowledge. Reich claimed that work democracy is beyond philosophy or politics; it is logical and functional, and at the heart of natural humanness. Work is also circular, with deep action learning reflection and renewal functions. In general, Social Enterprise practises subsidiarity, whereby decisions are taken by those nearest to the point of where a resolution is reached, except where the decisions affect other considerations within the organisation or its principles.

Problem 3   Exploitation and Low income

Low income bedevils working people the world over. It is a characteristic of capitalism, whereby the differential between the lowest-paid worker and the highest-paid worker is as great as the highest paid worker can get away with. It is also the cause of most industrial strife, and the amount of energy, time, resources, and bad feeling it generates is disproportionate to any benefit experienced by a small minority of top-paid workers. Astonishingly, the disparity continues in today's joined-up society, where unity is the keyword of every politician from the right or left in every election.

The idea that working people earn less than they can live on, and that the State uses taxpayers' money to subsidise the businesses that pay such low wages, is a ludicrous notion – especially when the companies make excessive profits. Capitalism prides itself on being a robust economic system, whereas in reality the below survival wages many pay to their workers, who then have to be subsidised by the State, belies that claim. Who would ever put forward such an idea? But it is a common practice in many countries. Undoubtedly, every business should pay a living wage, how otherwise can they be called viable businesses? They get away with it because the subsidy is to low paid workers, not the actual companies that maximise profit by not paying proper salaries. If the grant were paid directly to businesses, there would be a national outcry, and the demand that companies pay decent wages before profit-taking would soon attract attention. In a land of plenty, where the great majority of people have so little, something is fundamentally wrong.

Universal basic income is widely seen as a good thing, if only we could afford it. I'm not so sure. Unlike the National Health Service in the UK, basic income would not get universal support, it would always be part of the political toing and froing of all political parties. This endless boring topic of disagreement between them would, over time, cause political paralysis. It would mean that the State becomes much more critical and influential in everyone's lives. The government would forever be trying to reduce or shift the tax burden of the basic income, and the State would find that policing fairness and preventing cheating would create a whole new area of crime. Although it would undoubtedly fund some people who would use the time in creative ways, and might prevent homelessness to an extent, the bureaucratic intrusion into our lives, the overwhelming administrative backstopping, and the constant politicking would, in my opinion, outweigh any benefits that might occur. All State-run national programmes come with a host of restrictive conditions, especially when handing out money, which can only be administered by intrusive checks and balances, endangering personal privacy and moving towards nationalising conscience.

The shareholders' system of reward has always driven down salaries as an immediate and easy way to increase profits, and governments have tended to be too weak or too complicit to enforce a living wage. Universal Basic Income is no solution; if it were applied, it would always be exploited by the strongest in society – the corporations.

Solution 3   Financial viability

It is essential that every enterprise is financially viable – capable of being independent and in control of itself. But viability also has to be more than just making a financial profit, and must encompass being viable in terms of not exploiting co-owners/ workers, suppliers and customers, or the environment, in pursuit of trade.

Commercial viability is the resource required for human rights – the solution to low wages and poverty is to share the financial rewards equitably among those who create the wealth. In Social Enterprise, all workers are co-owners, and they decide on the wage levels they pay themselves. Profit-taking for the highest paid workers and shareholders does not exist. However, profit-taking for the co-owners does exist, and provides for proper levels of salaries and low- to non-pay differentials. As organic gardeners know, money is like manure: in a heap, it stinks; but spread around, everything grows.

Problem 4   Disconnect and apprehension

Being unconnected, not part of a community, and having no recourse to help and protection, is experienced as apprehension. The whittling away of 'society' and neighbourhood has been a continuous characteristic of the nature of global society. The replacement of 'common' facilities with paid-for services and the decline of local socialising, such as markets, pubs and cafes, youth clubs, community centres, piazza or town squares, churches and temples, parks and bathing areas, has curtailed social wealth. The ability for people to come together and organise, to share in opposing some threat, or creating new resources and celebrations to support opportunities, is diminishing or has gone.

Communication, connectivity, and socialising are now predominately online and out of our control. The very largest of corporations own and control the 'common spaces', the online platforms have replaced the cafes, parks, piazzas, etc. The accuracy and truth of what is communicated is becoming ever more questionable. False news is mixed with accurate news, and even elected politicians engage in exploiting this confusion to their advantage. What is real, and what is false, has become an everyday concern. The medium has ceased being a channel for communication; it has become the communicator.

Social media – part of large corporations' armoury – bombards individuals with information, advertisements, data, news, etc., but is not accountable and not transparent about how and why it chooses particular items to display. Who knows what they are not posting? People sign up to social media platforms, believing that they are communicating with a wide range of likeminded individuals. These online social bubbles exist not to ease connectivity, but to influence and sell merchandise. Where once online platforms held out a vision of future connections and social interaction, the interventions and usurping of the medium by corporations has led to an increasing degree of apprehension among those who use it the most – young people.

Under the canopy of such oppression, people are naturally apprehensive and are apt to respond to different types of powerlessness with impulsive behaviour. Crime is one, mental health issues another. Introversion and loneliness are also responses we see and can expect more of as the situation worsens. And often, it is the young who indulge, and increasingly believe in, conspiracy theories when truth and reality are skewed.

Solution 4   Social wealth creation

Social wealth creation means that through being connected, people can organise to create physical and human benefit together. Social Enterprise facilitates co-owners and stakeholders in building competencies and confidence in communication skills, as they are responsible for asking questions, listening, and explaining. It is essential that co-owners feel confident and able to express themselves, and are ready to listen to others expressing themselves. Part of this understands that some people are better and more articulate than other people, but all people have something to say. As most people work and live within defined communities of some sort, Social Enterprise can focus its contribution to invest in supporting connections and workers' competencies. This is done in a number of ways. First, the structure and process of co-owner engagement in governing Social Enterprise is about connections and personal improvements – through training and working together. Secondly, Social Enterprise interacts with suppliers in caring for the ultimate producer and their environment. Thirdly, some of its profits support community initiatives for the benefit of residents where the enterprise is based. And fourthly, its employment and procurement policies are inclusive, and in some Social Enterprises are proactive in recruiting people with particular needs. Social wealth drives Social Enterprise in equal measure, and with environmental responsibility combining the two, it enables local solutions to be found through communities working together in exercising robust responses and creative initiatives.

Problem 5   Environmental degradation

Environmental degradation is everyone's fault and everyone's responsibility. None more so than large organisations which, in addition to their staff's normal levels of pollution, are huge emitters of pollution. The way individuals pollute, and the way organisations pollute, are similar, but the scale is different, and the effect and impact are of an altogether different magnitude.

Underlying environmental degradation is due to the industrial revolution, which began in the 1760s with the extraction of fossil fuels, and the change from an agrarian and artisan economy to one dominated by industry and machine manufacturing. With it come the movement of rural populations to cities and the concentrated lifestyles still emerging around the world. Industries use our natural resources to produce technologies and goods in large volume that pollute and degrade the ecosystem and cause climate heating. But the alternative to produce less and change the technologies is held back by the capitalist economic system that is dependent on untrammelled growth. The dichotomy between slowing down natural resource use and associated polluting technologies, and the so-called need to speed up and expand growth, was the unresolved dilemma of the 20th century that has now worsened and become a crisis in the 21st century.

Growth should not be about accumulating rapidly to have more and bigger resources. In a finite world, this is an imbecilic idea; yet it persists and is choking us. The purpose of growth, in many instances, is not to satisfy a need but to maximise profit. In 1972, the report 'Limits to Growth' spelt out the results of unmitigated growth. Unfortunately, no-one in any governments or large corporations took any real notice, nothing happened, and growth continued to be the international metre of business and governments alike, worldwide. Limits to Growth was written 49 years ago, and today we are running out of fresh water, clean air, natural habitat, biodiversity, and human wellbeing. Years of wilful neglect have eroded our wisdom to counter the degenerative practices of governments and large businesses to such an extent that it is now adversely affecting society, the rule of law, neighbourliness, and individual wellbeing.

Our society is built on exploitative and degenerative commercial ideas and practices. This is not new, and we cannot blame anyone. It has just been the human way; use what is naturally available until it runs out, and then move on to something else. And, as Limits to Growth pointed out, this approach is not sustainable, and we have to check this and find alternative ways of thinking, doing, and being.

Movement in the universe is everything, as Einstein said: 'Life is like riding a bike, if you stop you lose your balance and fall off.' We keep moving and doing things, and up till now, we have understood this means growth in terms of 'more'. It was, perhaps still is, instinctive, but that doesn't mean it is right for our time. Because society has built its economic and social system around this instinctive urge to always focus on 'growth' in a simplistic and materialistic way of just 'more of', instead of being more enlightened and asking is it right to have more physical goods, will more of one thing degrade other things? Do we not want less of specific things to have growth in environmental wellbeing, for example? More iron ore, more coal, more steel, more cars are at the expense of more nature, more clean water, and more good air. Unselected and unfettered growth is now a danger to all of us. While this is clear, what is not clear is where to start changing from a growth strategy to a regenerative approach strategy.

In a finite environment, unlimited growth is unsustainable and inappropriate, but regeneration can sustain and is appropriate for our time. The growth model for the economy is designed to create volume, and the easiest way is to produce things that you throw away and then rebuy. The regenerative model is about producing stuff that lasts, and when worn out, can be revived, renewed, or recycled, in a circular economy.

Solution 5   Environmental responsibility

Environmental responsibility is the outcome of human rights – the solution to environmental degradation is for each enterprise and organisation to turn around the unintentional trend of degrading the environment to being a regenerative eco-action orientated organisation by design; being environmentally responsible in all its actions and materials. Environmental responsibility is an integral part of Social Enterprise; it is not an add-on and an additional cost, with all the additionality that brings, but at the very heart of the organisation.

The impact an organisation can have by reducing or achieving zero waste is significant, and yet the input required per person is much less than, for example, a family unit. Organisations need only make minor changes to have considerable impact, whereas individuals and community groups have to each make substantial changes to achieve the same pro-rata benefits. Manufacturing, transport, natural resource extraction, energy generation, wholesale and retailing, and construction, are all big polluters and producers of waste materials. A lot of this is down to the design, technologies, and methods used by our industries, who singularly focus on the single bottom line. Just take a couple of examples, all new building construction can easily be designed to have integrated south-facing slanting roofs, built entirely using photovoltaic solar materials instead of tiles made from slate or concrete. Often solar panels are retrofitted as an afterthought at a high cost, while the cost of building solar roofs in the original construction is negligible. In 1975, in the wholefood shop run by the commune Lifespan, we never used plastic bags or packaging. All customers were asked to bring their bags which, in our estimation, increased sales due to the favourable response by shoppers. There is no excuse for plastic bags, or constructing a building in old-fashioned ways, nor has there ever been – it's just lazy politics. Politicians may wonder why they are vilified, but it's simple: they don't do their job correctly and care for the planet and the people.

Organisations, businesses, and government departments are all in a position to behave environmentally responsibly in everything thing they do and impose on others to do. They have the wherewithal to rapidly move towards zero waste and renewable forms of heat and light. What they don't have is the will and intelligence to decide to behave correctly. As with many issues, it is the voluntary sector that initiates and advocates for sociocultural and environmental good practices and changes. The very organisations that have little influence or power have to trickle-up their ideas, which is, from experience, like pushing three cannonballs up a steep hill at the same time.

Problem 6 The financial bottom line and GDP

The fact that registered organisations only have to report on their financial income and expenditure and balance sheet enables them to exclude the social and environmental cost of running their businesses. These external costs are borne by the State and taxpayer. Paying benefits to those on low wages, cleaning up the environmental damage to the planet, and funding the care to cope with the emotional cost people tolerate in the often degrading hierarchical management command structures. Society and taxpayers bear these costs, and the benefits are expressed as additional profits for owners of assets.

In the old days, capitalists got away with maxims such as this one from Yorkshire: 'where there's muck, there's brass'. But today we know better than to allow such sentiment to excuse the destructive behaviour of capitalists, or do we? And if we don't, it's about time we did.

Solution 6 Social Accounting and Audit - the triple bottom line

Measuring performance builds trust for human rights – the solution is to impose the triple bottom line accounting practice, what is known as Social Accounting and Audit, to include, in addition to financial accounting, social wellbeing and environmentally responsible behaviour as part of an organisation's regular planning and measurement cycles. For these two additional values, a set of key performance indicators should be used as a minimum check on the health of each organisation.

Organisations, companies, and government departments all create pollution, and many have poor employment practices; they need to be more accountable for their actions. Just being accountable for their income and expenditure is inadequate. And even if they brag about their corporate social responsibility, we know from experience that this is just marketing hogwash. It is time to get real and include in their annual reporting and accounts how the business has reduced waste and pollution, and how it has increased social wellbeing. Regularly, every year, the triple bottom line must include planning, resources allocation, and results for the enterprise's financial, social, and environmental operations. Only then will we get change, and because corporate accounting is open to the public to view, customers can easily investigate and decide whether or not to do business with particular enterprises.

6 DEFINING SOCIAL ENTERPRISE

Social Enterprise is a form of a commercial enterprise where ownership, control, and wealth distribution are evenly spread, and people and the environment are an integral part of planning and accounting, leading to a more inclusive and fair organisational system. Social Enterprise is attractive to employees because they part-own and democratically control the enterprise and know that the use of any profits, from their labour, is under their control. It's also attractive to customers, as the value-added a customer receives from purchasing from a Social Enterprise is knowing that the organisation has acted responsibly, and the use of profits for social and environmental purposes is assured. Investors and trading partners also recognise the long-term viability, and will want to secure good working relations.

In the previous chapter, we looked at the problems and solutions that lead us to the six values enshrined in Social Enterprise. In this chapter, I want to build on the values to set out a definition of Social Enterprise.

Once defined, Social Enterprise would then represent a real entity that is recognised in law and by customers, traders, and co-owners. Establishing Social Enterprise in law through a Social Enterprise Act would create a visible entity, enabling it to function within the world of commerce and ethics. It would guarantee members their rights of ownership and control. Also, by formulating a definition that can be enshrined in law, investors, traders, customers, and public sector bodies would have clarity and legal recognition when doing business with Social Enterprises.

From the late 1970s, the following definition for Social Enterprise has been in use.

A social enterprise is a legally registered organisation owned and controlled by its members based on the values of equity in ownership. It trades commercially for financial independence and gain, creates social wealth and operates in an environmentally responsible manner. Social wealth and environmental responsibility are created as an integral part of Social Enterprise's operations or can be delivered through its profit distribution.

A Social Enterprise is measured by its success in achieving the triple bottom line of profitability, social wealth creation and environmentally responsible operations.

This definition was applied early during the 1980/90s in the UK, and to a lesser extent, in other parts of the world. Communication wasn't good and the message often got distorted, so the original definition was interpreted differently in different organisations and countries. There was no internet in those days; information on such topics was communicated via conferences, journals, or research papers. So for many people unaccustomed to these academic channels, there was little opportunity to be informed. The actual definition was challenging, and the rationale for Social Enterprise was less urgent then than now.

The original book on Social Enterprise contained the same values as expressed in this publication, but in a more holistic and rounded way. This book intends to articulate the values explicitly as the foundation for the Social Enterprise definition. Before the original book, the term Social Enterprise did not exist. I coined the term Social Enterprise to describe a new type of trading organisation designed for the 21st century. The new approach partly represented worker cooperatives that included viable trading, common ownership and democratic governance, with the addition of social wealth and ecological criteria when planning and accounting for performance, using an internal Social Accounting and Audit method as part of the annual financial audit.

How the six values of Social Enterprise link together and create a whole organisational structure.

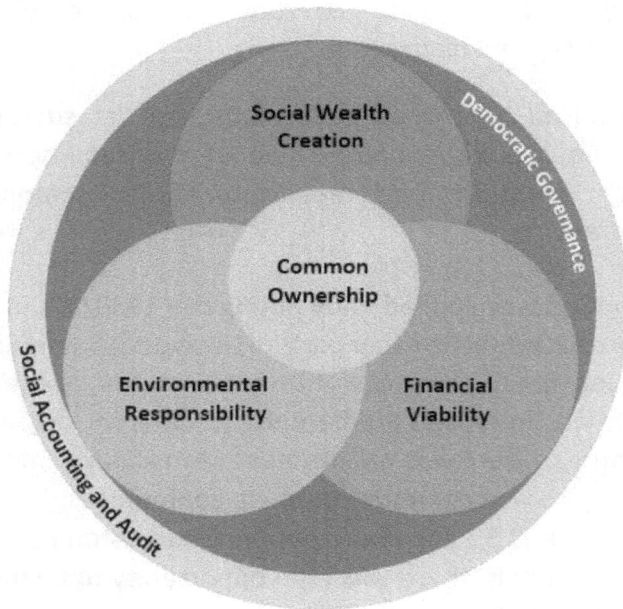

The Six Values for Social Enterprise

Value denotes importance, usefulness, and the measurement of exchange. In Social Enterprise, we use values to connect the big issues with concrete criteria and actions. Here we use values to make Social Enterprise relevant to today's situation. In the past, trading organisations had one value – to 'maximise profit' – and to our detriment, this has proven insufficient and allowed behaviours that have damaged society, people, and the ecology. To change this, we need to create new values for trading organisations that enhance and regenerate society and the environment. The use of values in Social Enterprise will be set first in the legal charter, to establish the culture of the enterprise; secondly, to set vision, policy, and targets; and thirdly, as criteria for planning and measuring performance. The combination of these values results in an emergent value of its own for which we as yet have little conceptual understanding and adequate measurement tools.

The six values that comprise the definition:
1. a legally registered organisation owned by its members/ co-owners, based on the values of equity in ownership
2. democratic governance and control – one co-owner one vote
3. an independent financial entity which trades viably
4. social wealth is created through the democratic practice of governance, and in the way the Social Enterprise interacts with its co-owners, customers, local community, and trading partners
5. environmental responsibility determines the way a Social Enterprise carries out its operations, and in the way it governs its supply and market chains
6. the Social Accounting and Audit system is used to plan and capture the results of the triple bottom line of financial, social, and environmental targets as part of the annual accounts and reporting

I use these values in a definition of Social Enterprise, but these have not always been adhered to, nor adequately recognised by those who support the general idea. One reason for this is my insistence in the late 1970s that the tripartite criteria for planning and measuring performance should be used voluntarily. I always thought that if it had been presented as mandatory, Social Enterprise would not have taken off. It would, I reasoned, be too challenging. I think I was right at the time. The many countries that provide support do so without a particularly clear and consistent definition. However, I now think that the flexibility afforded to different groups to define Social Enterprise is undermining the very essence of the benefits offered, and I believe it is time to press ahead with a legal definition. The global emergencies demand a Social Enterprise Act, with a supporting Social Accounting and Audit mechanism. Yet, even without an agreed definition, Social Enterprise has come a long way.

The concept of Social Enterprise has spawned many new inclusive operations, such as social impact measurement, social investment, the Social Value Act in the UK, Social Accounting and Audit, Community Interest Companies, social firms, community enterprise, etc. The concept minus the definition, I believe, facilitates this outpouring of 'social' organisational innovation. A strict definition early on may well have stifled much of this innovation and development, and led to a much-reduced impact.

The concept resulted in a global spread of new ideas and practices designed to make commercial and non-commercial organisations more responsive to 21st century challenges. We know the single bottom line is no longer adequate to plan strategy, make decisions, or measure performance. The world has become too inclusive and complex to think that all commercial endeavours are about extractive behaviour in terms of profit maximisation. All organisations, private and public, impact on society in some way; they are therefore responsible for knowing what the impact is and doing all they can to mitigate any detrimental effects when and where it occurs.

Social Enterprise is part of the solution to today's major problems. In the world, we face multiple problems that seem to emanate from two key systemic causes: limited asset ownership and control, and the financial bottom line measurement criteria.

Since its inception in 1978, Social Enterprise has always focused on six key values. These were present in the 1970s, but are now much more pressing.

6.1 Value One – Common Ownership

Common ownership guarantees the rights of those who create wealth to determine how it is used.

The value of a legally registered common ownership organisation is that all workers and, in some cases, volunteers are co-owners. In community Social Enterprises, local residents are co-owners. Common ownership is based on the belief that if we own an equal share of the enterprise, we will gain the most from our physical and mental inputs, and be more engaged in and responsible for how we organise and plan our operations and behaviour. Common ownership ensures those who invest their labour the highest return on their investment. If it is imperative to break the stranglehold of inequality imposed by corporate capitalism, the structural alternative is to have shared ownership of assets by the greatest number of people.

The principle of common ownership by co-owners of a Social Enterprise means that each member holds one equal valued share, and has one equal vote in decision-making. Common ownership by co-owners underpins the democracy and equity that distinguishes Social Enterprise from private/corporate business.

Registered common ownership embeds the legal structure within a truly humanist ethic. People and communities need to acquire ownership of assets, land, and patent rights, to have the power and control to self-determine their lives and the lives of future generations. There is evidence that many of those early pioneers of Social Enterprise from the 1970s/80s, that legally registered their collectives as common ownership, have survived and thrived, while those who worked in someone else's enterprise, which pretended to be a Social Enterprise based on 'goodwill', have subsequently withered or gone bust. Unless ownership is in the hands of members, there is no real change, there is just goodwill, and after time that goodwill breaks down and then there is only private ownership.

Since the signing of Magna Carta eight hundred years ago, ownership in the UK is the stuff of ultimate power, control, and benefit. Who owns controls, who controls makes decisions, and those who make decisions do so in their favour.

In Social Enterprises, shares have two purposes: one is to legally register ownership over the Social Enterprise and all its assets by co-owners; and the other is to confer a financial value to the co-owners. Individuals can own an equity share of the total value of an enterprise as in a joint-stock company, or they can be a non-equity shareholder, where the value of an enterprise is held by the members collectively. In the UK, this type of structure is a company limited by guarantee, whereby co-owners guarantee to pay the nominal sum of £1 in the event of the Social Enterprise being wound up.

Common Ownership confers:

- responsibility and status
- control of profit distribution and investment
- control of purpose and direction
- self-esteem
- equality

Until there is a 'real' change of ownership, it is unlikely that there will be any real change in the way businesses operate or why they are established.

6.2 Value Two – Democratic Governance

Democratic governance guarantees the rights of every co-owner to express their opinion on any topic.

The value of democratic governance, based on being a co-owner, is to have an equal vote and say on the decisions the organisations make. Having an equal and legally binding vote in the democratic governance of planning and working together increases people's confidence and self-esteem, their learning and capacity building, as well as finding the best answers to any work-related questions. To have an educated and knowledgeable workforce to run our enterprises, work democracy is the least costly and most effective way we have at our disposal. The decisions made at the level of governance can and may decide to deepen democracy and devolve decision-making to other levels, engaging more co-owners in the process of work democracy.

'Work is rational, politics, mysticism, and ideology, are irrational; therefore, why not use work as the democratic basis of our governance system?'[11] If work is rational and logical, if we have things to do, then it is not beyond our ability to organise the way we do it for the benefit of those doing the work and for the benefit of sustaining the enterprise. Democracy is developed through learning to work together and share in decision-making and resource allocation. Empowerment of co-owners, through involvement in the governance, will lead to personal and family improvement, and work enjoyment, best practice, and care for the local community in which the enterprise is based.

Can people work, make decisions, and achieve in a non-hierarchical organisational structure? Up to this time in our

---

[11]   William Reich explored the notion of work democracy as an antidote to the rise of fascism in Germany in The Mass Psychology of Fascism.

evolutionary development, the answer has been no. Hierarchies dominate our family life, school and college structures, work environment, recreational activities, and social circles. History tells us about the politicians, business titans, and criminals who succeed in crawling their way up a hierarchical system.

Hierarchy measures levels in vertical order; it is a very useful way to structure all manner of ideas and systems, everything from filing documents, arranging strategic plans, and preparing shopping lists. It always means a superior and an inferior, or a cause and effect; it is perhaps the most used system of classification in the world. There is even something instinctively natural about the order of hierarchy. But it can also be misleading. Singular and exclusive hierarchy is a simple concept that is increasingly too easy to apply where a situation is much more complex and requires a correspondingly complex approach. Hierarchy, especially when used in organisations of people, can be stifling in the way it excludes the ideas, experiences, and innovations of the very people who have a lot to offer. In addition, it is often demeaning, not necessarily on a personal basis, but in the structure of the hierarchy. We are still, for example, struggling with the ancient hierarchy between men and women in many aspects of our so-called 'enlightened' society.

In today's complex world full of 'variables', we need multiple layers of thought, ideas, and innovations. Organisations without hierarchy are seen as disorganised, anarchistic, chaotic, etc. The word has come to symbolise order, calm, efficiency, where everyone knows their place. In reality, we see many hierarchical structures in turmoil; we see companies go bankrupt due to mismanagement at the top; we see countries floundering because of the leader's fear and loathing; we see organisations, nations, and even empires lose their way, as supreme leaders lose theirs. And we see leaders who fulfil all that is expected of them. The point is that hierarchy is no guarantee of success, any more than flat organisational structures.

There is no absolute type of organisational structure. We choose our structure, and because Social Enterprise is co-owned by the workers, they are bound to choose systems to make the enterprise succeed, and that makes working an enjoyable experience. In Social Enterprise, we recognise the need for flatter organisational structures that take account of many individuals' points of view, where any issue is dealt with in an inclusive manner.

No one Social Enterprise is the same, but they do tend to use a three-tier system of organisational management: governance, team management, and operational self-management. All tiers use democratic decision-making, but each tier is likely to range from full voting at the governance level, team working at the operational level, and self-management at the task level.

Decision-making

In a hierarchy, an individual is an ultimate authority and arbitrator in decision-making, and we trust in their wisdom and individual knowledge to know best. In teams, we rely on group decision-making after having discussed and explored the options. The concern with teams is that members of the group can be materially compromised by not agreeing on technical options, and are evenly split between two or more options. Or one member of the team is in a personal dispute with another member, and cannot bring him/herself to support that person. These circumstances are often cited as reasons for having a single hierarchical final arbitrator. However, it can equally be said that, by having a single arbitrator, that individual can also be caught in the same type of traps; they too can be technically undecided and unsure of the 'right' options, or personal preferences or biases can psychologically compromise them. Leaders can make terrible choices, and sometimes are unable to take advice due to their status, and cannot be seen as equivocal. At least with teams, there is room for members to change their opinion in response to collectively exploring, in some detail, all the options available.

The efficiency of circular organisations is immeasurably greater than hierarchical structures. Everyone knows what is going on, communication is instantaneous, and opportunities for feedback and review abound. When a decision is made, everyone knows as much as anyone else, and everything is transparent. Also, inclusive decision-making tends to be more strategic than exclusive decision-making; the process of iteration means a decision has had the benefit of being critiqued by different people from different positions in the organisation. The balance between the team and a self-managing individual's decision-making is the combination of trust and respect. The team has to trust an individual in appropriate circumstances to make decisions that they would support if they were on hand. An individual has to respect and anticipate the team's level of support when making decisions in areas of their responsibility. The process of subsidiarity is the principle that a team should have a subsidiary function, performing only those tasks which cannot be performed at a more local level by an individual. The team, however, is responsible for creating trust and respect among its group, to ensure confidence in individuals to make decisions.

Democracy and Decision-making involves:
- different points of view aired
- risks identified, options developed, different aspects brought together and combined
- working with others and learning

- focus on efficient and comfortable meetings in work time
- always having the right to vote on every decision
- the chairing of meetings is rotated
- discussions and decisions of meetings are recorded

Working together means learning and practising what is learned; sharing jobs with others requires being both a leader and part of a team; rotating tasks invigorates the practice of work; and being a decision-maker and a follower of others' decision broadens the understanding and instils a sense of worth for each member. Work experience in Social Enterprise prepares members for career development, whether in their place of work, or if they wish to move on by using the multiple skill base they acquire as the basis for new experiences and work opportunities.

Work democracy, based on the rationality of getting tasks done, is dynamic, interactive, urgent, and critically spawns good decisions; it is eminently superior to the dead weight of hierarchy.

6.3 Value Three – Financial Viability

Financial viability guarantees independence and freedom of choice for co-owners.

Financial viability, based on the commercial exchanging of goods and services, enables an organisation to be independent and experience fuller control over its decision-making. The basis of financial viability is straightforward; it means to trade to make a profit over and above the costs to produce and service that work. Profit and loss measurement is well established, and every trading entity is obliged by law to report their financial transactions annually.

Being viable is being independent within a market economy where people and legal entities can freely trade and earn their livelihoods, without interference by the State or other organisations. Viability will also sustain the independence of the enterprise as individual co-owners come and go.

Social Enterprise operates in the macroeconomic system, as private business does. It can borrow money, can sell non-equity shares (a debenture stock), and it can use financial mechanisms to arrange favourable trade terms. It also has to pay the same tax and national insurance, and can arrange pension schemes for staff. Although it pays the same fiscal costs and fulfils the same borrowing criteria as a private company, it also invests more in internal training and job rotation. Social Enterprise pays more to the nation's wellbeing than a private company, due to some of the profits being reinvested in external social and environmental initiatives.

Social Enterprise can be a mixed receipt organisation; it can receive earned income from sales, and receive grant funding for specific social and environmental projects, not dissimilar from private business in general. However, because it proactively intends to improve the social and ecological aspects, grant support is an important option.

The significant difference is the ability to decide on the pay structure and how profits are used. Social Enterprises tend to pay higher salaries than those in the private sector. It is not unknown for them to pay the same hourly rate to all workers, regardless of role and tasks. Most, however, do pay different salaries, but keep the differential to a low of one-to-three, unlike in many large UK companies where senior staff's pay can be as high as over 100 times the average worker's pay.

Aspects of financial viability:

- trade for profit and pay taxes
- reinvest profits in the organisation and/or use it for social and environmental purposes

- can reduce prices for some customers, based on their need
- can increase expenditure to foster and achieve the social and environmental principles
- can provide dividends to co-owners

How profits are distributed is up to the co-owners to decide, and how much is allocated to different areas. To impose rigid structures on profit use would be anti-trade, and not be relevant to some Social Enterprise and even adverse to others. It is advisable, however, to set the policy on apportionment for how profits are distributed well before profits are made. Profits are usually distributed in four ways: reinvestment in the commercial side of the enterprise; dividends for co-owners; to a reserve fund; and, donations made to social and environmental benefits/projects.

6.4 Value Four – Social Wealth Creation

Social wealth guarantees transparency and opportunities for co-owners and others to work together and create benefit for themselves and society.

Social wealth creation is the backbone of society; it refers to the functioning of groups of people, and includes interpersonal relationships, shared identity, shared norms and values, leading to trust, cooperation, and reciprocity. Social wealth creation is the enhancement of individuals, families, and communities, through co-operating and coming together. Social Enterprises enable social wealth creation through common ownership, democracy, supply chain care, and the use of financial surpluses to support community wellbeing. Social wealth creation fulfils psychological and interpersonal relationship needs. It facilitates shared solutions to problems, whether they are local loss of facilities, environmental damage or biodiversity loss, people having disputes, or any number of issues which, if people come together, can be solved. The ability and wherewithal to connect and share will be one of the significant assets of the mid-21st century, and may even be the kernel for a new beginning.

Common ownership and democratic control allow the enterprise to design, within the organisational structure, conditions to support communication between workers and between workers and external stakeholders. Support for networking, group mobility, visits and study tours, and engagement in a wide range of interactive commercial and social gatherings, is part of social wealth creation. Training and rotating work roles and tasks are often used in Social Enterprise to enhance social wealth and opportunities for co-owners. The investment in training to skill up staff to rotate tasks and responsibilities improves the quality and enjoyment of workers' experiences, and supports them to grow as people. Multiple skilled workers are also more adept at helping others in their community, as well as helping themselves advance their career prospects. Co-owners can arrange to volunteer in local projects or care service as part of their paid work, and at the same time, enhance the standing of the Social Enterprise in the community.

Purchasing directly from small-scale producers, Fairtrade agreements, networking with suppliers and trade customers, and in joint investment initiatives, enhances communication and idea exchange. Trading locally helps the money circulate and, through the multiplier effect where the same Pound/Euro gets spent a number of times, enhances the local economy.

Trust among people is further enhanced if they share common interests. Social Enterprise's democratic governance prepares people to enter into discussion and decide on important issues such as how to spend the financial profit, how to support the local community, and how to improve biodiversity. These and other important areas create a platform for debate, learning, and decision-making that can have a powerful influence on building trust and mutual aid more widely in the community – both online and face-to-face.

Social wealth creation involves:

- being part of a community
- integrating social care and actions into operational duties
- good governance of the enterprise
- operating Fairtrade in its supply chain
- donating surplus profits to good causes and projects
- volunteering and connectivity

6.5 Value Five – Environmental Responsibility

Environmental responsibility guarantees the regeneration of the natural world and the biosphere.

Being environmentally responsible in our work and the organisation enhances biodiversity, reduces waste, and improves the quality and quantity of soil, air, and water availability. It's also, today, good business. The easiest way to positively affect the environment is for organisations to adopt zero waste and zero operational emissions practices, and human behaviour that integrates with the commercial operations.

The more knowledgeable we are about the harmful effects of doing business, the more aware and responsible we are becoming. Responsible environmental practices can sometimes be financially more costly and take longer to operate, and this should become the standard expectation of doing business and running organisations, and not seen as an additional cost or considered as external. Social Enterprises often set organisational policy to financially invest in ways that reduce their carbon footprint and reduce harmful emissions and the amount of waste they produce. They have a responsibility to enhance environmental wellbeing through managing energy use, materials, transport, and processes, in regenerative ways that create least waste and pollution and actually sustain and, where possible, enhance biodiversity, soil, and water qualities.

It is all very well for individuals, families, and communities to reduce waste and recycle more, but all this is irrelevant if business and industry ignore environmental responsibility. The world is being rocked by the consequences of human-caused climate change. The political and corporate response is ineffectual, and frankly in denial. Every individual, business, public body, and nation is responsible for curbing the cause of climate change. We must not be deceived into believing we individuals must be the only ones to do the planet-saving stuff. Businesses, whatever their size, are the ones that need to take responsibility. If businesses stop wasting resources on packaging, so will we; if energy companies source their power from renewables, so will we; if retail outlets stop using plastic bags, so will we; and if transport companies stop using oil, so will we. What organisations and businesses do impacts on society and the environment to a much greater extent than what individuals and families do.

Environmental responsibility:

- considers how every trade agreement and investment affects the environment and biodiversity
- invests in regenerative technologies, methods of operation; organisational systems are measured using financial and social audits on their commercial, social, and environmental performance
- manages supply chains in line with good environmental standards

- integrates physical operations and human behaviour within a mindset of regenerative approaches by design

Environmentally responsible action involves everything, starting with the legally binding constitutional statement of purpose to policies, strategic planning, design of process, investments, type of equipment and machinery, training, and marketing. Environmental responsibility has to become the default organisational position, on a par with financial probity. Individually, every one of us has to be responsible for our actions; every small action, if it's done in a way towards zero waste and frugal use of finite resources, is eco-action. Individuals and organisations, in one respect, are the same. They have to change their way of doing things now, not later. We don't have time for that. Since the 1960s, I'm aware that hippies and scientists have been alerting the public and politicians to overpopulation, too much use of fossil fuels, air pollution, land and water misuse, climate warming, and environmental degradation. And now, of course, our children are scolding adults for wasting resources and polluting the planet. It is time for regenerative eco-action to become the guiding principle in our planning, design, and creation.

Regenerative planning and action is when an organisation integrates and enhances skills, relationships, and confidence of the individuals involved; when we use a material resource, we always complete the task by establishing the process of replenishing the resource or offsetting the damage through investment in other biodiversity actions; when we pollute air-water-soil, reforestation must be supported and invested in. The simple rule of thumb is: when we chop a tree down, always plant two in its place. Expression of this value can engender customer trust and increase sales, while reducing environmental costs to the state and society.

6.6 Value Six – Social Accounting and Audit and the Triple Bottom Line

Social Accounting and Audit guarantees transparency and the means to plan, monitor, and achieve the triple bottom line values.

Social Accounting and Audit is the organisational method used to combine the planning and measuring of financial, social, and environmental operations in a Social Enterprise. By law, companies have to present their audited accounts for annual public scrutiny. In Social Enterprise, the annual statements also include social wealth creation and environmentally responsible operations; at present, this is voluntary. Still, the longer governments delay action on the environment and on the high levels of inequality in society, the more urgent the triple bottom line accounting becomes. This may well lead to new laws making social and environmental performance measurement accountability legally compulsory, along with financial reporting.

Using the triple bottom line or tripartite criteria of financial viability, social wealth creation, and environmental responsibility, establishes appropriate criteria against which to plan, implement, and evaluate enterprise performance. Achieving these engenders a sense of esteem by co-owners of their achievements. The easiest way for organisations to switch from the irresponsible financial bottom line to a tripartite bottom line is to integrate the triple criteria in the planning and design of the operations, with clear indicators and assumptions for measuring the results.

Planning and measuring results in Social Enterprise are variously called "Social Accounting and Audit' (social audit). Over the years, this process has gone through several permutations, some complex and some simple. Unlike corporate business, Social Enterprise plans are as much about change as about target planning, and more about the six values than profit maximisation. The process of measurement has to be administratively integral to work, not as an add-on but as part of the everyday operations. It has to be realistic and fundamentally useful.

At present, there is little appetite for compulsory Social Accounting and Audit, and those who use it do so voluntarily, even if not always wholly. A social audit system uses an internal sliding scale scorecard around issues such as: personal wellbeing, ownership, democracy, and profit distribution; traditional financial accounting methods; an adapted international standard project planning method of the 'Theory of Change'; combined with internal and external stakeholder surveys.

It is necessary to plan for the desired results of the six values that combine to create the value to achieve whole worth outcomes and impact. Planning is used to provide direction and to engage with co-owners and stakeholders creatively and thoughtfully. Planning is also a crucial part of learning to improve the quality of operations. The process measures actual performance against the plans, and this enables managers and co-owners to know what is working well and what is not, as well as reinforcing the learning of how to best govern and manage the enterprise.

Planning engages co-owners in a participative governance approach. Engaging co-owners in the planning process not only attracts a lot more ideas and understanding to help the organisation achieve, but it is also an excellent way to keep everyone informed and up-to-date on what is happening and why a particular plan, as opposed to other options, was chosen. People are diverse in their capabilities, and it is always surprising and rewarding to witness individuals as they find their place in an organisation. Initially, many people are unsure or shy about their skills or interests, and the process of planning is an excellent starting point for exploring their place within the enterprise. Planning offers co-owners opportunities to see where their particular interests and expertise can be applied, and how they can get involved in the broader governance of the enterprise or even focus on specific areas that interest them.

Planning is indispensable; it is the start of the action learning cycle, and leads the practical operations of creating goods and selling services. There are degrees of planning: the whole organisation does long-term strategic planning through the governance mechanism; operational plans will be detailed and have targets and milestones, accompanied by indicators, and have thorough annual reviews carried out by management and/ or work teams; whereas, short-term plans will be detailed and action-focused with time and result indicators, and be monitored quarterly by co-owners. All plans should be linked, with short-term planning being practical interpretations of medium-term plans, and in turn, medium-term plans should be how to implement the strategy. All plans should have measurement indicators – some more detailed than others – and accompanying assumptions to understand the external risk factors.

Planning is cyclical; once started, it never ends. Monitoring and evaluation reviews, however, punctuate the process. These will be quarterly, as well as annual reviews, with occasional strategy reviews and planning over extended periods. Planning concerns governance as well as management, so it is valuable to engage as many people as is appropriate and realistic, keeping in mind that in addition to face-to-face meetings, communication can be supplemented by online systems.

In Social Enterprise, measurement is a learning tool and is primarily used to improve the process and quality of operations. The analysis from the measurement results provide data to account to stakeholders, and to demonstrate the audit trail to show how the results were arrived at, as well as to prove their accuracy. The process of planning, implementing, and measuring is a fundamental action learning tool that Social Enterprises apply as part of their organisational and democratic system.

The value of measurement is in understanding how any result was arrived at. Too often, external consultants are called in to undertake the measurement process, denying the co-owners the full knowledge of how and precisely where in the process weaknesses were identified, and improvements recommended. Many improvements can be made at the time and place where weaknesses are identified, if co-owners do the measurement as an integral part of their work, rather than wait for the year end to receive a lengthy report from external consultants. If the planning and targets are well structured, measurement is mostly based on simple planned and actual variance analysis. If co-owners know how to spot any variances, they can act quickly to put things right and achieve the target on time and within budget. Or if the weakness is a significant problem, they can bring it to the attention of colleagues at the earliest opportunity, to deal with it appropriately. Learning lessons is a key output of measurement, but too often the lessons learned are only on paper and fail to be converted into implemented solutions – mainly as a result of the divergence of external monitors/auditors' position and perception from those who carry out the operational functions. If co-owners, however, monitor themselves as an integral part of the operations, then lessons learned can be applied immediately by the very people who identified the weakness. Where self-monitoring happens, it will still be necessary for an external auditor to verify the results, audit trail, and conclusions. When reporting on the Social Accounting and Audit, having an external evaluator to verify the results is essential in building confidence amongst stakeholders and officials. If a Social Enterprise wishes to use the results of the measurement as a form of accountability to customers or the general public, they will need to provide the full audit trail and/or have their results independently verified to instil trust in the results reported.

Social Accounting and Audit involves:
- planning together
- setting milestone and targets
- measuring and improving at work
- learning lessons
- accounting actual progress/result and knowing 'what's going on'
- measuring success and failure
- applying learning and improvement
- being accountable and transparent

7 THE ORGANISATION OF SOCIAL ENTERPRISE

Social Enterprise organisation has to reflect the six values in the way it is structured and in the way it carries out its operations. The legal charter adopted should comprise the six values at the level of ownership and democratic rights and policy statements; beyond that, it is up to the way the co-owners decide to structure and manage the enterprise, especially how decisions are made, and by whom. It is vital to have the flexibility to try out different systems in work planning, task allocation, decision-making, and accountability. The excitement and thrill of working in Social Enterprise is not so much in the products and service, but in the way co-owners can experience being fully alive and important.

The legal charter is half the organisation; the internal management structure, how operational functions are arranged, lines of authority, and decision-making, is the other half. The legal charter, once signed off, can be changed but does require 75% voting in favour, which then needs registering with the authorising government-appointed body. Although this is not too onerous, it is nonetheless something rarely done. Hence, the charter has to be broad enough to enable co-owners lots of room to try out different methods of the internal organisation, without overstepping the boundary of the legal constitution. In addition to the standard charter regulations on ownership, voting rights, and the need for financial probity, Social Enterprises also take on enabling social wealth creation and environmental responsibility as an integral part in their operations. Furthermore, to include the social and environmental responsibilities, it is necessary to add the Social Accounting and Audit system requirement to integrate social wealth creation and environmental responsibility in the management planning and annual reviews.

The legal charter will state all six values in broad terms, and it will be the Governance Body which interprets these general statements into operational rules and processes. This gives considerable authority to the Governance Body to experiment with organisational structures and systems. In some Social Enterprises I've worked in, when they introduce a new method or system, they give it time to test and review before deciding whether to adopt it or not, before embedding the change permanently. It has been important not to allow new methods to drift, but to fix a future date by which time it should be possible to make a positive decision on maintaining the new idea, adjusting and maintaining it, or abandoning the approach and reverting to the original method. If decisions are not allowed to drift, everyone is involved and knowledgeable as to the result of trying new ideas; without this accountability, there is no learning.

Social Enterprise practises circular organisational systems and structures, not always absolutely and not always perfectly. Moving from a hierarchical system to a circular system takes time and learning. The six values provide the basis for an excellent circular organisation: common ownership = equality; democracy = the right to voice opinion; financial viability = the need to work together; social wealth creation = care for colleagues; environmental responsibility = care for the environment; and, Social Accounting and Audit = being open and honest. These values should not only influence the enterprise's organisational structure, but in addition the structure should reflect the values in the way the organisation behaves in its daily operations and with its external stakeholders.

There are always contradictions in any human organisational system, and while we may try to iron them out, we shouldn't be surprised or accusing if a few persist. Let's recognise them and learn from them, and always try to create integrity where possible. Democracy and efficiency still collide, and occasionally compromise is necessary. Being democratic means that anyone who holds authority over other people or processes will also be subject to the collective authority of those over whom they have authority. And while this may not be keenly felt in the daily operations, it is nonetheless a dichotomy that has to be worked with and learned from. In circular organisations, it is often less about a manager managing people and tasks, and more about managing processes and relationships within the organisation and with trading partners, advisers, and local communities.

A Social Enterprise organisation has four main broad functions, with control resting in the common ownership structure. Ownership determines who ultimately controls the organisation and how decisions are made, and who else, besides the employees, is involved. Within the overall control exercised by co-owners, the Governance Body decides policies, aims and objectives, organisational rules, strategy, planning, investment, organisational systems and accountability. Management and Workgroups are responsible for implementing the governance plans, day-to-day decision-making, and daily financial and administrative operations. Operational functions are undertaken by teams which produce and deliver the goods and services. Individual co-owners/staff are self-managed members of teams, responsible for carrying out the operational role and task functions in the interest of the enterprise. How the precise organisational structure functions will vary considerably, and is dependent on the technical operations, scale and size of the workforce, and the values adopted by the co-owners.

What is meant by a circular organisation in Social Enterprise?

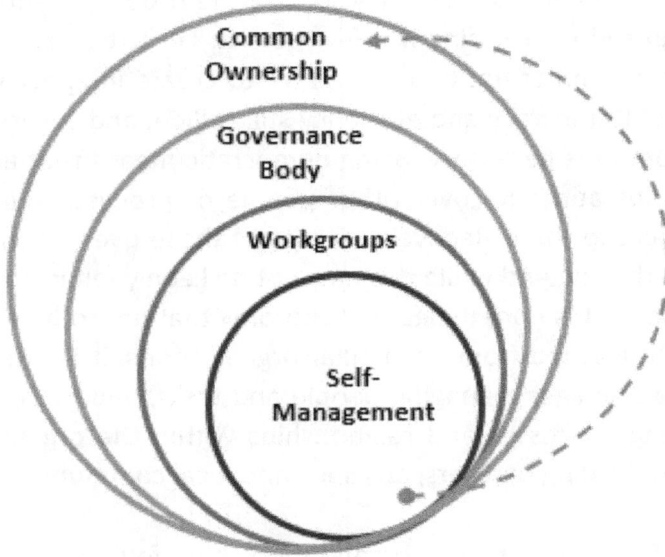

7.1 Common Ownership

Legally registered common ownership establishes the basic rights of co-owners. It means that everyone who creates the wealth of an enterprise and contributes to its sound management and responsible behaviour, is the beneficiary of the wealth generated.

Co-owners are employees of trading Social Enterprises, and in community enterprises can also be residents of a specific geographic area. But in such circumstances, compulsory co-ownership cannot apply to residents; their involvement must be voluntary. In a trading Social Enterprise, it is part of the terms and conditions of employment that all workers are automatically a co-owner as well. There may also be particular circumstances when a Social Enterprise forms a partnership with other organisations and companies, and may wish to design their charter to allow an additional corporate co-ownership category.

The way private business is organised reflects the ownership structure; those with most shares have the most significant say, exercised through a command-and-control hierarchy. It is just a normal way of running the enterprise. In Social Enterprise, where no-one has more power than anyone else, a vertical structure has to be operated for other reasons, if at all.

Who can be a co-owner of Social Enterprises is decided upon and written in the legal charter which sets out the process for recruiting members, their roles and responsibilities, their entitlements, and how they cease being a member. Common ownership is equivalent to shareholding without the financial cost or reward. Co-owners of the Social Enterprise can either have no financial stake in the enterprise, which is then owned collectively by all co-owners in common (called common ownership), or co-owners can have a financial stake in the enterprise as an employee co-owner, sometimes called employee ownership.

The specific form of co-ownership will be stated in the Memorandum of Association of a legal charter, where the rights and responsibilities of a co-owner are defined. All Social Enterprises have workers as co-owners, who automatically become a registered member on formally being employed. This usually means that the worker has undertaken a probationary period working for the enterprise before being officially offered the job and membership. As part of the Terms and Conditions of employment, and supported by the legal charter, workers automatically cease being a member on terminating their contract of employment. In my experience, when a Social Enterprise selects to offer employees co-ownership status as an option, and not part of the terms and conditions of employment, it erodes the collective spirit if and when employees opt out. It creates a two-tier organisation of co-owners and employees.

In some cases, employee-owned enterprises enable employees to accumulate financial stakes in the enterprise through annual profit distribution issued in debenture stock[12] that do not carry additional voting rights, or a system of A and B shares, where A shares holds the ownership and one vote, and the B share holds accumulated financial value with no voting rights. Regardless of the amount of financial investment a member has made, their vote is still one member one vote.

In the case of community enterprise, external members are usually local residents; for traditional retail co-operatives, external members are customers and trading partners; and for organisations like football clubs, members are the fans. There are also marketing co-operatives where co-owners are trading partners, such as agricultural producers. Common ownership should always be designed to suit the circumstances of the Social Enterprise, with the proviso that co-owners – whoever they are – only have one vote. The level of involvement by co-owners in managing the enterprise should aim to increase as the organisation matures. As co-owners learn and gain confidence, their participation is expected to increase and deepen. The presumption is that greater involvement leads to greater satisfaction – self-management by the largest number of co-owners in governance and strategy planning.

Common factors are:

- common ownership must be legally registered
- each co-owner only has one vote in the decision-making process
- only co-owners can be owners of the Social Enterprise

---

[12] A debenture stock in the UK is a preferential loan that in the event of bankruptcy is repaid with interest prior to other repayments such as tax and trading obligations, but do not carry extra voting rights.

- workers cease being co-owners on termination of their employment contract, or in the event of other categories their co-ownership status ceases in relation to the cessation clause in their charter

7.2 Governance Body

The Governance Body is made up of co-owners, and sets policy, investment decisions, hiring and firing decisions, operational strategy and planning, profit allocation, and manage the Social Accounting and Audit as well as the financial audit. In small enterprises, all co-owners are members of the Governance Body, but in bigger organisations efficiency means that the face-to-face discussions have to be limited to a reasonable number of co-owners who rotate the responsibility. With the use of online technology, all co-owners will have access to viewing the proceedings of meetings. By using online voting and discussion platforms, important areas can easily be communicated to the entire membership and, if needed, discussed and voted on by everyone.

The Governance Body in a Social Enterprise is the leading authority from which all other lines of authority emanate. Governance in Social Enterprise is the process of representing the co-owner's interests in the role of overseeing the enterprise in all its operations. All co-owners of the governing body have fiduciary duties in legal, financial, and business responsibilities on behalf of external stakeholders.

The UK Government's seven principles of public life for civil servants might also fit well within Social Enterprise, if interpreted in this way:

1. Selflessness
Co-owners should act solely in terms of the financial, social, and environmental interest of the enterprise.

2. Integrity
Co-owners must avoid placing themselves under any obligation to people or organisations that might try inappropriately to influence them in their work. They should not act or take decisions in order to gain financial or other material benefits for themselves, their family, or their friends. They must declare and resolve any interests and relationships.

3. Objectivity
Co-owners must act and take decisions impartially, fairly, and on merit, using the best evidence and without discrimination or bias.

4. Accountability
Co-owners are accountable to the public for their decisions and actions, and must submit themselves to the scrutiny necessary to ensure this.

5. Openness
Co-owners should act and take decisions in an open and transparent manner. Information should not be withheld from the public, unless there are clear and lawful reasons for so doing.

6. Honesty
Co-owners should be truthful.

7. Leadership
Co-owners should exhibit these principles in their own behaviour. They should actively promote and robustly support the principles, and be willing to challenge poor behaviour wherever it occurs.

If the organisation is large, then too many co-owners would make it unwieldy to manage, and some form of representative structure is required at one level – similar to a shareholder board in private companies, but different because the co-owners, unlike a shareholder board, are the workers and have a more intricate knowledge of the workings of the enterprise. Co-owners have direct experience of how the organisation works and its capacity, and are also the ones who will have to implement any decisions made. Decisions made at this level, however, are more likely to be strategic than operational, and longer-term.

The composition of the governing body is, of course, dependent on the size, technical operational sector, and expertise needed for decision-making, and on whether the organisation operates a hierarchical system or a team-based system of revolving tasks and functions. Whatever system, it is essential to have the governing body representatives appointed on a rotating basis. A principal value of Social Enterprise is for co-owners to experience being both leaders and led. This will enable the entire workforce to learn, through 'lived experience', how the roles are conducted, and the knowledge necessary to perform the tasks of governance. A simple rule of thumb is for the governing body to retire one-third or one-fifth of its representatives annually, thus, keeping everyone involved, learning and contributing ideas, and experiencing long-term planning and short-term daily work tasks.

The type of organisational structure not only depends on the size, technical operations, and the skill sets required, but has to reflect the shared ownership status of each co-owner. For example, some enterprises operate traditional management systems equivalent to a corporate board representing members, who employ staff paid according to their seniority in the management structure. In others, there is more participative democracy in the way management devolves responsibility, and where staff are paid the same and manage the enterprise through a series of working groups. Each Social Enterprise is at liberty to determine its organisational structure and management system. In some sectors, such as transport and warehousing, where skills are similar, it is relatively easy to learn and rotate tasks, but not so easy in others, such as pharmaceutical or large-scale engineering enterprises. In general, though, the structure (legal and procedural) should be as flat as is possible to enable co-owners to be involved and gain benefit, and instil self-management. Staff rotation, training, and opportunities for innovation should be built into the organisational structure, and these should be part of the consideration when planning the enterprise.

Many Social Enterprises emphasise the need for co-owners to be involved in several areas, from daily work to governance, and social and environmental initiatives. To facilitate co-owners' engagement, Social Enterprises invest time and resources in training to fulfil these responsibilities. In a sense, all workers are apprentices in self-management, as few people will have been formally trained in non-hierarchical systems. Not only will this investment reward Social Enterprise in being well governed and managed, but also provide interesting working conditions and career paths for co-owners. The central learning for co-owners is that decisions are made in the interests of the enterprise, as well as for themselves. This separation between the individual and group is at the core of good governance, and must set a new type of professional behaviour.

Co-owners, who are involved in both management and menial tasks, know what is happening and why. This openness and accountability contrasts with vertical-structured organisations that tend to be secretive, citing the reason for withholding information and plans as a way to guard against competitors poaching their ideas. But in many cases, secrecy is primarily to enable senior management to hold onto their position and status – knowledge is power. All commercial companies, to a degree, need to safeguard their plans and innovation, so a balance between openness within the organisation and the need for protective secrecy is down to each enterprise's unique situation.

Hierarchy is a fantastic way to order ideas, things, and plans; it is also an efficient way to organise people, when either they don't mind or there is good reason, such as a short-term emergency. The overlap of organising people and plans in hierarchical ways is altogether very powerful. Using hierarchy to structure ideas and plans needs to be separated from using it to organise people in self-managing organisations. Team working and self-management is how we as people develop, learn, and prosper, whereas hierarchy deadens people's enthusiasm and erodes their efforts to contribute ideas and insights to a degree where no learning takes place. How we organise work is partly dependent on the level of technical expertise needed in the enterprise; there are technical decisions, management and strategy investment decisions, governance decisions, and daily task decisions.

Social Enterprise will have stakeholders; these are individuals and organisations that have a stake in the proper running of the enterprise. How a Social Enterprise treats and interacts with stakeholders is a matter of concern. They can be very supportive and helpful, or antagonistic and undermining. Stakeholders comprise customers, suppliers, residents where the enterprise is located, local government, co-owners and their families, who can all have an influence on the enterprise or who are influenced by the enterprise. As part of scoping for the annual Social Accounting and Audit exercises, stakeholders will form the external review. Their involvement and their views and comments are an essential part of good governance. The more stakeholders like the enterprise, the better the business it will conduct.

The organisation, management, and regular running of the operations are all greatly enhanced if the enterprise's intentions, aims, and objectives are clear. In Social Enterprise, we use the Governance Statement; this document is initially drafted by the Governance Body, and agreed upon by the co-owners. The Governance Statement summarises the enterprise's purpose and modus operandi, and is used to set criteria for the Social Accounting and Audit system.[13] All organisational processes and decisions will, in many respects, be self-evident thereafter. The Governance Statement will guide the organisation and the decision-making for the commercial, social, and environmental plans, and will be reviewed and, if necessary, updated annually.

The Governance Statement will explain the purpose and structure of the Social Enterprise and determine how it should operate, and should comprise the following statements:

- Value Base – how the Social Enterprise applies the six values, according to their sector and environment
- Main Aims – these should reflect the Memorandum and Articles of Association in the legal charter, and indicate the trading operations objectives, the Social Wealth Creation intentions, and Environmental Responsibility adopted by the enterprise
- Policies – list the policies; some will be statutory, and others can be prepared to reflect the Social Enterprise's values and indicate where they can be viewed
- Operational Objectives – these will describe the commercial aims and objectives in detail
- Organisational Rules – these will be decided on during the running of the enterprise, and written in the minutes, and they should then be transferred to a Rule Book

---

[13] See Social Accounting and Audit Toolkit 2020.

The financial, social, and environmental aims and objectives should align with the statements in the Memorandum of Association in the legal charter that will have been drawn up for the Social Enterprise at its inception. Stating these in both the Governance Statement and in the constitutional charter makes it much easier for the enterprise to legitimately claim tax deductible expenditure on any costs associated with furthering their social and environmental aims. These will then form the operational guidance, and can be useful in positioning the enterprise as part of marketing. The main duties of the Governance Body are:

- define the Social Enterprise
- set policies, strategy, and long-term investment plans
- review and update plans regularly
- oversee the Financial and Social Accounting and Audit
- be accountable to a wide range of stakeholders
- set operational goals
- respond to and deal with disputes and other problem areas

The Role of Governance and the Role of Management

Social Enterprises are managed in two ways: the first is via the co-ownership, which has overall responsibility for the governance of the enterprise; and the second is the operational management undertaken by appointed and paid staff (who are also co-owners).

Co-owners use the Governance Statement to guide the management of the enterprise, which is agreed by all the co-owners at their annual general meeting (AGM). It does not involve itself with operational issues, but defines expectations, grants powers, prepares organisational roles, and verifies performance. Operational management responsibility is delegated to workgroups, managers, and self-managed co-owners.

The biggest challenge facing Social Enterprise is the old-fashioned concept that organisational forms have to be rigidly hierarchical. Social Enterprise is different; it aims to alter the way people own, control, and benefit from work; it aims to create inclusive methods of organisation. Inclusive forms of organisation are when co-owners are enabled to be involved in areas of responsibility and work. Sometimes, they are the same, and other times, they require different skills and approaches. Inclusiveness will create a sense of security, where individuals can initiate discussion, plans, and innovations, and feel free to support other individuals in doing the same.

Openness is the key to functioning democracy and self-management, and often reduces the need for sophisticated discretion on whom and what is discussed. There are occasions for discretion when discussing individuals' behaviour and when planning commercial strategies. But by and large, openness leads to more people knowing what and why something is happening, and that enhances co-owners' sense of participation and worth. Being secretive, on the other hand, leads to frustration and a feeling of being undervalued and irrelevant. Self-management does mean that although we use traditional terms such as manager, governance, committee, etc., people cross over these boundaries frequently when being both a manager and operational worker, for example, or when co-owners rotate tasks, roles, and responsibilities. One day you are doing the accounts, and the next you're driving the lorry. That's what makes the experience of working in Social Enterprise so interesting and rewarding.

7.3 Management and Workgroups

Departments, units, teams, are all descriptions of how organisations describe workgroups. Workgroups carry out the tasks and activities of an organisation, whether they are office-based, working in a factory, or service providers, but most work in some form of groups. Sometimes they have managers, and other times they work collectively. These workgroups will themselves come together in coordinating the whole enterprise's operations, sometimes with a manager or representative board. Often there are individuals, sometimes called managers, whose responsibility is to oversee the relationships within the group, and between the group and other parts of the enterprise.

There are three essential policy choices for managing a Social Enterprise. First is the major decision focusing on organisational structure; management can have a hierarchy of authority and responsibility, or it can choose to manage by a series of working groups — each one managing a specific part, and together managing the whole enterprise. The second main policy is on salaries; are co-owners paid the same for different jobs, or do they have wage differentials? The third is about tasks and roles' rotation; in many Social Enterprises, they are rotated at some level, depending on the degree of self-management practised.

In between the Governance Body and the co-owners' self-management lies the management and coordination of processes, tasks, and workgroups. This middle tier of the organisation can be structured similarly to many companies by having 'middle management' coordinate all the functions and relationships, and performing a hierarchical control and command role; or as teams of co-owners who carry out the daily tasks and also manage their workgroup and the functional processes, and coordinate the different relationships both internally and, where appropriate, externally. Typical workgroups are, for example, an administration group, a marketing group, a transport group, a manufacturing group, an IT group, etc. These groups often rotate tasks, similar to the Governance Body, with one-third retiring and joining another group on a year or two-yearly basis. Also sometimes, because of expertise or other reasons, a person can be involved in two or more workgroups.

Management is the function of coordinating several different things to achieve one objective. This function is traditionally performed in a single pyramid-style hierarchy, where one of a few individuals has the authority to tell everyone else in the organisation what to do. Those not part of the top echelons of management cannot question that authority. This approach presupposes that there are only a few individuals with the capacity to understand and direct what happens. If there were more people involved, it might, so the argument goes, lead to disagreements, confusion, and poor management. But our personal experience is that this is a nonsense idea; we know from our own family, community, school, university, politics, Social Enterprise, etc., that many people are quite competent to manage things. And we know that those at the top are sometimes actually less competent, and make bad decisions and then impose them on other people. Having to do something useless or silly just because your boss says so, challenges our sense of wellbeing and diminishes our enthusiasm for work. Being the boss is a source of immense pride or stress, and being part of a group of bosses lessens both the satisfaction and stress but increases social wealth and wellbeing. I've heard it said that equality is the 'suppression of difference'. From my viewpoint, equality is the liberation from the strictures of hierarchy and the opportunity for creative expression. The adopted style of equality in Social Enterprise is not the suppression of the individual, but the creative opportunity for them to excel.

As a general rule, Social Enterprise divides overall governance by co-owners from operational management by fewer co-owners. This can be hierarchical, it can be through rotating roles and tasks, or it can be by core groups assigned with specific decision-making responsibilities. Whatever system of management is used, the intention is always to move towards self-management, even in hierarchical or teams; co-owners need to take responsibility for their work and the enterprise. Self-management can take time for people to get used to, either because of low confidence or conversely overzealous personality traits. Either way, we need to learn how to be responsible for our actions as individuals and as teams.

Wage parity is a radical idea and practised by a small number of Social Enterprises, but most use wage differentials and keep the levels low. Commonly the highest-paid is only three times that of the lowest-paid. Especially for wage parity enterprises, many workers receive considerable in-house training so they can alternate tasks and roles, working in the same position for a few months or longer in some cases at a time, and then revolving to another area. The benefit of this approach is twofold: the work is more varied and interesting; and workers are highly trained in several business and technical skills. This approach works easiest in low-skilled sectors, such as retailing, warehousing, transport, back-office services, and much lower skill manufacturing, whereas industries such as pharmaceutical, aviation, IT programming, etc., are less able to share roles and tasks. However, this is a decision each Social Enterprise has to take, usually at its inception, because once a decision to pay differential salaries or parity salaries is made, it is a difficult decision to change. So this needs careful consideration.

The opportunity for co-owners to be trained in different areas is part of the social wealth creation, as well as being part of developing new ways of working. All co-owners need to learn essential management and chairing skills, the responsibilities of being an owner of a limited liability company, democratic practices, how to read accounts, and about the triple bottom line accounting. Also, there will be specific technical skills needed to participate in the main commercial activities, and there should be an opportunity for co-owners to learn, in-depth, particular skills that would benefit the enterprise and themselves.

Running an organisation structured around the six values, and carrying out the Social Accounting and Audit as the method of planning and measurement, is not to be found in business schools. It will take some time yet for them to catch up. For the time being, it is necessary to learn on the job. Action learning – the cycle of coming up with an idea, implementing and testing the idea in a controlled way, reviewing and measuring results, learning lessons and applying new learning – facilitates individual and group learning. In a task-orientated environment, this approach is both realistic and rewarding, for groups or teams, and is especially apt as a self-learning tool.

There are two fundamental areas where co-owners need to know and understand why they should be involved. One area is marketing – planning the sales volume and selling the goods or services to buyers; and the second area is finance – planning income and expenditure, and maintaining proper records of financial transactions, and regular reporting on sales income and expenditure.

Marketing is about getting the mix of product/service, location, price, and the customer communication right, and in Social Enterprise this will still be necessary. Marketing has often been seen as the ugly face of business, being disingenuous with the truth, and flogging customers things they don't want by the use of tricks and treats. Social Enterprise has to continuously attract a growing customer base and, because of the values enshrined, the way it does that is to use transparent and honest approaches with all its stakeholders, especially the way it informs customers of what's on offer, making sure that the product/ service is of high quality and is sourced from reputable suppliers. Marketing can be used by Social Enterprise to communicate the six values, and in doing so, expose the poor quality and bad practices of competitors.

Proper financial management is critical for running any business, and like any business, Social Enterprise has to make a profit. Because of the legal requirement that every company anywhere in the world is obliged by law to keep proper accounts and submit them annually to the government-appointed authorising body, they tend to be managed accurately and kept up-to-date. In Social Enterprise, there is an additional requirement of financial transparency. Every co-owner is entitled to see the accounts at any time. Because co-owners are those who will ultimately make financial decisions, the more they know, the better that decision-making will be. Commercial confidentiality is part of every enterprise, and co-owners, just like private business shareholders, must respect and understand the need for withholding financial information from the general public and competitors. At the end of each fiscal year, this information is submitted in a proper and orderly manner for inspection; it will be available for the public to see, in the form of audited financial accounts.

7.4 Self-Management

Co-owners can be empowered by both carrying out tasks and being responsible for tasks. Their role is more than an owner, more than a worker, and more than a manager. Combined, it enables them to translate experience and knowledge into a new category of worker – the self-managed person. Being part of a workgroup, a self-managed person can, when needed, call upon colleagues for assistance, guidance, and mutual problem-solving, thus creating a self-sustaining environment in which the whole enterprise benefits. The self-esteem experienced by co-owners is one of the most critical aspects of social wealth creation.

Many workers' co-operatives and communes use working teams to organise, manage, and implement tasks. At Lifespan Community, any individual who has the expertise or who has an idea can lead a team of others, yet at the same time remains a part of a team led by someone else. This sharing of roles and responsibilities is empowering and efficient, and leads to new learning and insights into decision-making and capacity building. Working at the level of aligned self-managed teams is better served if workers are paid the same hourly salary rate, as happens in some Social Enterprises. One significant result of self-management is that decisions can and are made at the point of implementation. The efficiency gained and the time saved means that when discussing actions at meetings, it is less about making decisions and more about what decisions were made, why, and what were the results. In this way, the lessons learned are shared, and can be applied immediately to the next team task.

In Social Enterprise, the intention is to move towards self-management. Here, I refer to self-management as 'acting on your own or with others on behalf of the interests of the group and organisation'. Self-management is an act of individuality; it is from the individual that inspires work for service to others and the self. Coercion cannot achieve self-management; the group is not the driver but the enabler of self-management, and each person has to find it in themselves to be responsible. Working for the group as well as for yourself, and being both a leader and a team member, is hugely satisfying. We have to enjoy the creative experience of self-management; making decisions and acting on them fulfils basic instincts of personal worth. We feel more of a real person if we are responsible for our actions, and if we can work in accordance with what we think is best for ourselves and the group. Sometimes this means taking a risk, both for the individual and the group. To make this work, the group has to recognise and support risk-taking. Any entrepreneur or scientist will understand that risk is necessary and rewarding, but on occasions backfires. Co-owners have to be mindful of the organisation's purpose, objectives, and interests. This includes recognising where and when to draw the line, and to defer the matter in question to the relevant group for wider consideration before taking action. Self-management implies knowing your limitation, and in an enabling organisation, this is seen as a strength, not a weakness.

The six values provide the basis for measuring performance in many ways, thus creating a learning organisation that is always growing in its ability to regenerate finance, people, and the planet. Action learning is at the heart of Social Enterprise. The six values all contribute to a healthy organisation, and they all offer co-owners areas of interest. As different people find different ideas of interest, the opportunities for co-owners to engage in something they're interested in and that will enable the enterprise to function better and be more successful, is a function of self-management.

Organisational change will come about if people are emotionally flexible and dextrous, and democratic organisations work when those involved can see others' views alongside their own, however difficult that may be. Self-management is needed for each person to be responsible, to see, and then to act. To think in terms of everything is ours, we own it and are responsible for its good governance, without question. However, being a co-owner is no guarantee to being responsible; it is the building block to being conscientious. Social Enterprise needs to build attraction, a safe place and opportunity so co-owners pay attention to what is happening and, in their own and others' interests, self-manage where appropriate.

7.5 Meetings and Decision-Making

We often hear people say that talking is good. Talking helps individuals and groups learn, understand, and see things differently. This helps us recognise how others see the same thing. Talking helps individuals see themselves more clearly, and talking helps people through painful emotional experiences. So let's talk. The meeting, if chaired well, is an excellent and safe place to talk. Meetings run Social Enterprise, and everyone must learn about chairing, listening, and speaking in meetings.

Meeting is the hub of Social Enterprise organisation and management. Meetings can be awful and go on too long, be fractious, and not get much done, or meetings can be dynamic, places where people are informed, learn, gain confidence, make decisions, and are invigorated. It depends on the structure, chairing, and how responsible participants are in focusing on the topic on hand. Ultimately, the meeting must be fun, serious, and efficient, all at the same time.

A meeting is when people formally come together to discuss and decide on some topic or topics. As a function of work, they must be professionally conducted, with responsible chairing, agenda and minutes, and they should operate a quorum of some sort. Meetings are also places where groups of people come together to discuss and theorise about future possibilities where no decision is being made. These are designated non-decision-making – for discussion only.

An important lesson for all co-owners to learn is to recognise that a meeting, more than any other place, is where individuals listen and talk and give and take. Once people experience 'giving in' and not always being 'right', even if they remain convinced of their own position, the group experiences a sense of wellbeing. This is when a meeting changes from being a place of dread to a place of fun; by giving a little, the team benefits a lot.

Enforcing a time limit on a meeting is a simple and effective way of focusing on what needs to be done. Half an hour is short, and two hours is a long meeting. If the chair sets a time limit of somewhere in between, then meetings will function well. Participants who go on too much will be cut short by other participants who are more interested in the topic than listening to somebody repeat themselves. The chair is responsible for getting the meeting done on time, by allocating time for each topic on the agenda. It is surprising how effective a time limit is in concentrating participants' mind on the task.

Chairing meetings needs practice; people can learn to chair a meeting well if they take the task seriously and act professionally. The best way of doing this is to rotate the role of the chair, so everyone gets a chance to learn how to behave – both leading a meeting and being a participant. In this way, the chair is not a power role, and it does not come with added knowledge or authority. It is a task that lasts as long as the meeting lasts, and then a different person is automatically chosen to chair the next meeting. At Summerhill School, children as young as eight start chairing the weekly meetings, and these usually include all children and adults, with upward of 80 in attendance. The chair of each meeting rotates the task to another child. Spreading the opportunity in this way is a form of action learning in being both a leader and follower on a regular basis, and is a powerful learning experience.

As a function of work and not a social gathering, attendees need to adjust their personal relationships to other attendees;

they must act as a worker of the enterprise, and not as a friend or foe. This is critical. It's important that all co-owners help create a culture of professionalism, put aside their personal relations with other participants, and adopt the position of supporting or opposing an issue based on their viewpoint, not on who they like or dislike. In many Social Enterprises, rotating the task of chair is common practice.

Voting versus consensus: voting is about getting the topic done with a clear and final decision, whereas consensus is about getting everyone to agree on a decision. These methods are mutually exclusive unless different topics are discussed with different decision-making methods. In most work situations, there is neither the time nor the need to use consensus decision-making; although, in meetings about governance or strategic planning, a more consensual way is maybe needed. However, my personal view is always to have the right to vote to finalise each decision. From my experience of living and working in co-operative organisations, as long as the meeting is well chaired, it becomes the preferred management system of the enterprise – it is also where equality is exercised and experienced.

At every point of decision-making in the enterprise, there is a corollary of accountability that must run through the organisation, like veins in the body connecting it all together. Decision-making and accountability are different sides of the same coin; one without the other invalidates both, and is often the cause of discontent in organisations. Every time a decision is made, it is the responsibility of those deciding to make sure it is widely known and understood within the organisation.

7.6 Planning

Planning is a continuous process. Once the enterprise is up and running, the original planning documents will become the start of the ongoing annual review and planning process, guiding the enterprise, and becoming part of the governance statement for measuring performance. This process is usually overseen by the Governance Body, and should engage with all co-owners and be ratified by them each year. As planning is the beginning of the process and accountability the end, it should always be seen as cyclical, where they are linked and at the beginning and end of each cycle. The cyclical nature of planning and review creates a corporate method of action learning. The original plan used after one year of trading as part of an annual review of performance, and the results of the analysis, should inform the planning for the next period – the process of planning and reviewing is ongoing, and one of the most informative exercises an enterprise undertakes. A plan should cover a period of three to five years, and state the practical steps required to achieve the planned objectives; this is broken down into periods of one year, with annual financial information. This is referred to as medium-term planning. Strategic planning can cover a period of up to ten years, with less emphasis on the practical steps necessary to achieve the plan, and more emphasis on having an agreed long-term aim that guides the operations and short-term decision-making.

Participation by all co-owners in the planning and review process ensures democracy, transparency, and accountability. How this is done varies, depending on the numbers of co-owners. In small groups, a good way is to run facilitated workshops; in bigger groups, a mixture of online sliding scale question sets, and facilitated live question and answer workshops.

Planning is the process of trying to work out where in the future you want to be, and how to get there – the planning process itself is halfway to getting there. The process is used to test if an idea is financially viable, socially and environmentally responsible. Planning is also a way of bringing together a potential group of co-owners when starting a Social Enterprise to develop the organisation and learn about business methods. The information gathered is written as a feasibility study and planning document, which will be part of the governance statement, and also used to attract investment and other forms of support. It is also the opportunity for the group to make a judgement on the likely success of implementing the plan, and to determine the values that will be central to the enterprise. This form of action learning builds confidence, and being involved in decision-making empowers members, as owners, to be responsible for their actions – planning is an essential mechanism for making common ownership work. The planning will also test the main aims and culture of the enterprise, and question if the aims are still relevant and viable, and if the culture of the common ownership and democracy is working well.

Accountability to all stakeholders is a fundamental characteristic of Social Enterprise. The way management is carried out, the Social Accounting and Audit system, engaging with suppliers and customers, and the general openness of how business plans and operates, provides the way for a new type of transparent organisation.

8 SOCIAL ACCOUNTING AND AUDIT

Initially developed in the 1970s, the primary system and criteria for the Social Accounting and Audit method have remained intact. Improvements to the techniques and processes, however, have been incorporated. It wasn't until 1978, when Social Accounting and Audit was developed as a regular internal procedure for enterprises to set their objectives and measure against their indicators, that the concept became widely applicable. Social Accounting and Audit was initially designed for Social Enterprises to incorporate financial, social, and ecological performance – now known as the triple bottom line – in planning and evaluating ongoing operations. It also engaged with stakeholders in soliciting their views as to the plans for, and results of, performance. The Social Accounting and Audit system was the first non-financial internal organisational measurement method. It was originally designed and used to be participatory and transparent, and undertaken by the organisation using its own values' and objectives' criteria. Before this period, social measurement in trading organisations had only been used as a one-off evaluation on selected criteria, or carried out by external bodies attempting to expose malpractice in certain industries.

Since that time, a number of other methods have been developed. There is Social Impact, which uses the theory of change to set targets in a hierarchy of progressive levels of achievement, and measures each level against the final horizon. Then there is the Scorecard, which is a simple method of using a set of questions, against which to score performance on a sliding scale. Social Return on Investment, a form of cost benefit analysis, has been used when converting social benefit or cost into financial indicators, and is then included into the financial accounts. Corporate Social Responsibility is used in many large corporations as part of their annual reporting to shareholders, focusing mainly on their internal legal compliance. In the development sector, methods such as Planned and Actual, Cost-benefit analysis, Results Based Management, and the Theory of Change, are some of the most widely used planning and measurement approaches.

There are many more methods; each has its pros and cons. Depending on the particular questions that need answers, specific techniques will also be selected for their accuracy. Each Social Enterprise will have to investigate suitable systems and choose one that meets its needs. The original method developed in 1978 is Social Accounting and Audit, which is designed as a management planning and performance measurement tool, and as accountability and reporting tool, in that order. This method was never intended to 'police' a Social Enterprise, but to help it improve all-round performance, which is why it was presented, at that time, as a voluntary exercise.

Commercial organisations must undertake financial accounting to determine their performance and value. There is an entire industry of accountants and chartered accountants dedicated to accounting; they are so good that they can apply the letter of the law while circumnavigating the spirit of the law. Financial accounting focuses exclusively on the income and expenditure and asset values to explain performance for a period, and overall value of the enterprise. This data is then aggregated by central government to form the basis of Gross Domestic Production (GDP), which in turn values a country's worth. The implication of this approach is to value people, organisations, regions, and countries, solely in financial terms. The balance between income and expenditure, and the value of the plus or minus of owned assets, is variously known as the single bottom line, and takes no account of external non-financial costs and benefits. There is, of course, no reason why measurement should not be segmented, otherwise it would not be useful for analysis and planning. But to measure the performance of a trading organisation that uses a range of non-financial resources, and creates additional and external pollution, and interacts with a range of external stakeholders in both positive and negative ways, is to belie the value it espouses.

If the financial values do not reflect the actual cost of the performance – such as the cost to the environment, human and emotional damage, and the cost of overexploitation of finite resources – then does this type of measurement and value mean anything real? For example, it is possible, using GDP, to say that South Korea is one of the top wealthiest countries in the world, yet it is also number three for male and female suicide rates in the world. China represents the second largest economy in the world, whilst being the number one environmental polluter in the world. The US is the number one economy, and has a high level of institutional racism; and the UK is the fifth largest economy, and has one of the highest rates of child poverty in the world. So, what do these values mean any more? Does it mean that by having a strong economy, there must be human and environmental exploitation and sacrifices? And if so, what does that say about a society that discounts social and environmental values?

The UK's Joint Stock Companies Act 1844 was soon followed in 1855 with the general Limited Liability Act that cemented the use of the financial bottom line as the sole form of measurement for all business. Since then, 164 years later, nothing much has changed in evaluating commercial operations. However, during the 164 years, a lot has evolved in the nature and scale of business transactions and, more importantly, in our understanding of the broader impact of commercial operations on the environment, social wellbeing, human health, equality, and the very survival of homo sapiens.

If we continue to use such an outdated and misleading indicator as the financial bottom line to measure performance and provide evidence for policymaking, then we must expect the continuing exploitation of humans and the environment to be sustained. It is time to step up and acknowledge what we know to be true: that the financial bottom line is woefully inadequate. There is no intention to do away with business, trade, or competition. It is just that the 'level playing field' of all companies having to measure performance based on their financial bottom line needs to be upgraded and modernised to encompass a wider remit of the cost/benefit of human wellbeing, resource use, and waste produced, to achieve commercial success.

The term and idea of Social Enterprise is predicated on widening the definition of meaningful and responsible performance. Without the use of broader values to determine performance, the idea has little purpose. In 1978, the term Social Enterprise was developed to describe a commercial organisation that used financial viability, social wealth creation, and environmental responsibility as the underlying criteria for measuring performance. Including two fundamental areas that commercial organisations make use of, but do not pay for, has become fashionable, but unfortunately not functional. The costs of social and human inequality and environmental degradation are exploited to achieve the financial bottom line, and the cost is still borne by society, not the enterprises. Both of these additional criteria represent the good of society and the existential threat to society; therefore, they must be factored in when deciding investments and outputs. Value for money is no longer enough; rather, is the investment going to create social wealth and regenerative outcomes, in addition to the profit of selling the goods or services?

In the 1970s, people complained that the burden on business, having to consider and account for these additional responsibilities, was too much. Apart from a very few individual companies, no organisation applied the internal system of Social Accounting and Audit. Although I protested and explained that the internal Social Accounting and Audit process need not be burdensome or complicated, I was soon drowned out by the academic clamour for detailed research and complex mathematical systems. If you were to try and scare off busy people from applying new measurement methods, being swamped by academic researchers writing detailed papers might be the easiest way. I argued, at the time, that Social Accounting and Audit was not an academic but a pragmatic approach to finding alternative ways to measuring corporate performance.

The intention at that time was for workers' cooperatives to apply Social Accounting and Audit incrementally and on a voluntary basis. Partly, it must be said, because many of the workers cooperatives were already investing in social and environmental externalities. But they were not measuring these investments nor presenting the excellent work in their accounts as both a positive contribution and a possible tax rebate. They were accounting only for their financial bottom line, and because they were pioneering new sectors and innovative ways of organisation and caring for the environment, profit margins tended to be low. Yet they already had extra commercial objectives, such as promoting recycling and renewable energy, changing diet by using more wholefoods, paying all workers the same hourly rate. These needed to be accounted for and used to offset the low financial profits. To achieve these extra commercial objectives, they should, so some argued, be part of the annual planning and investment strategy, and be included at the end-of-year measurement in an extended planned and actual process. Instead of planning and measuring the single bottom line, we should plan and measure the tripartite bottom lines.

As to the complexity of using the triple bottom line, in the workers' cooperative wholefood shop I worked in during the late 1970s, we paid equal wages to all workers, meeting our social wealth objective, and engaged customers in recycling packaging and not using plastic bags. We also collaborated with our supplier, Suma Wholefoods Workers Cooperative, to make sure we only bought goods from reputable countries with minimum supply chains, to enhance the income of the farmer producers. This, at the time, was more complicated than you might think.

The internal Social Accounting and Audit system was designed to be simple, focused, and pragmatic – doing what you can rather than pretending to do more while doing less. I was also mindful of what Einstein once said: 'Not everything that counts can be measured. Not everything that can be measured counts.' Each enterprise contributes a little bit, was the idea; what would the planet have looked like today had every company stopped using plastic bags in the early 1980s? For example, it was well known within the wholefood sector that plastic bags were bad for the environment, and in many shops were not used. The absurd thing is that, in practice, it was straightforward; we just insisted on using paper bags, and I might add, it was extremely simple paying parity wages.

The act of including social wealth creation and environmentally responsible behaviour is not difficult technically, financially, or in human resources and skills; the act of actually doing good is about making decisions to do so. We can hide behind an array of fabricated excuses to explain why we refuse to change our behaviour, but we know that is a lie. Of course, we can improve our behaviour. As I write this, the UK government, like many others 40 years too late, is finally in 2021 banning plastic bags and everyone now is bringing a bag with them to the shops. The horse has bolted, and now we are closing the stable door, and the oceans, fields, and towns, are full of plastic waste. The lessons learned are to plan, put in the details, budget, and highlight the human competency needs. If every enterprise does their bit, the change will be profound.

Social Accounting and Audit is not so much about the methodology as about actually doing it: putting the idea, target, or objective in the plan, attaching a few simple indicators, and measuring the results. The Social Accounting and Audit has to become part of the management system, in the same way as the financial accounting system is part of management.

Financial auditing is required by law; Social Accounting and Audit is undertaken voluntarily and should be done, primarily, to assist Social Enterprises in achieving their stated objectives and fulfilling their values. It is sometimes considered burdensome to have to measure non-financial performance. In reality, however, nearly all organisations do it to some extent, and it is more efficient to conduct a Social Accounting and Audit than to try to plan, implement, and be accountable in other ways.

Social Accounting and Audit enables organisations to explore and generate their values, which form the basis for setting criteria for measuring performance; these are recorded in the Governance Statement. Social and environmental measurement criteria are generalised to cover universal areas, such as gender and ethnicity equality, and reuse and recycle waste. Social and environmental criteria can also be specific to an individual enterprise and its physical location. We can, therefore, expect that enterprises will have to formulate their criteria for particular purposes relating to their trade and circumstances to complement generalised measurement criteria.

Even with a single action, the result often has multiple impacts. The use of a single method of measurement is misleading, because a single action – building a road, changing a law, stopping using a medication, or providing childcare – leads inevitably to multiple results. A new road affects people living alongside it – animals, the environment, and other users of roads; a change of law affects the judiciary, police, law firms, victims, and perpetrators, and society's relationship with the State; ceasing to use a medication includes the Ministry of Health, Ministry of Finance, hospitals, doctors, nurses, patients, and information processes; and when childcare is provided, it helps create healthy children, and enables parents to earn more income and companies to recruit more women. When an organisation includes the triple bottom line, it can be said that it is planning and measuring its performance in the round, or 'rounded', moving from a single bottom line to multiple bottom lines, to a rounded planning and measuring approach. This does not mean that it takes the three components of social, finance, and environment as parallel plans and audits. It moves beyond the three and combines them into one, an integrated hybrid of the three – the whole is greater than the sum of its parts. The hybrid could be singular in practice. You might plan the development of a physical product, and attached to that plan will be social, financial, and environmental considerations, along with more traditional concerns about markets, machinery, skills, etc. However, these will be subsumed into the three components of financial, social, and environmental, as they represent the apex of impact and benefit, which need planning and measuring corporately. It will provide a coherent and clear image of an organisation, and the planning and execution of all objectives transparently and fairly. A Social Accounting and Audit gives equal weighting to the triple bottom line objectives, and it is for each Social Enterprise to determine the levels of enquiry. This depends on the needs of the enterprise and the ability and interest of co-owners. Social Enterprises, when starting to use a social measurement, should begin by using a core and limited system, and build it up over a few years as co-owners become more skilled, and the auditing process becomes more integrated as part of the regular planning and review process.

Individual organisations can set criteria that relate to their stated purpose, including their immediate surroundings and their stakeholder relationships, to customise the Social Accounting and Audit to their own needs. It ensures performance is transparent, and enables the enterprise to identify, control, and report on successes and irregularities. And it provides the learning of how to develop Social Enterprises and how to create new values of benefit. Because it is undertaken voluntarily, it should be of benefit to the organisation. A Social Enterprise should find its optional level of process and detail to enable it to be effective and efficient. It should also provide greater understanding, for its stakeholders, of how the organisation operates.

If the enterprise is to achieve the triple bottom line objectives, it is essential to have in place some form of measurement mechanism that corresponds to those aspirations. Unless these areas are measured, they cannot be proved, and the worth of the Social Enterprise will be in doubt. It is constrained in the way it describes the purpose and how it plans its operations if it only uses financial accounting and audit measurement indicators. Sometimes they can be integrated into the operations of the Social Enterprise, and other times they are external and are supported through profit distribution and labour contributions in terms of projects.

Social and environmental planning and measurement should, however, be intentional. It should first and foremost provide the organisation with management information and learning on its performance, and then as a method for reporting and being accountable to stakeholders. Whichever approach is used, it should be undertaken regularly (i.e. every year or two years), should use the same methods each time, and apply the results and learning to the next round of planning.

Financial independence, social wealth creation, and environmental responsibility should guide the planning operations and be the criteria for measuring the combined performance. Over the years, I have tightened up the structure to make it more usable. Below is an outline of the Social Accounting and Audit system. I think the process should be undertaken by a small team of co-owners and, at least, one outside person under the direction of the Governance Body. They may well invite in additional people for some of the exercises. The description below is an outline of the process and exercises used. Please go to the Local Livelihoods[14] website to download a free copy of the Social Accounting and Audit Toolkit for a complete explanation.

Preparing a Governance Statement

The Governance Statement is part of the Social Accounting and Audit processes as much as a standalone statement about the enterprise. The Governance Statement sets the main aims, operational objectives, policies, organisational rules, and value base. These comprise and specify the six values in more detail,

---

[14] www.locallivelihoods.com to download a free copy of the Social Accounting and Audit Toolkit

to be used as criteria for measuring performance in the Social Accounting and Audit process. This document is prepared by the Governance Body, or delegated Audit Team, and provides the guiding statement for managing the organisation.

The Position Analysis for the Social Accounting and Audit

Typically, positioning a business refers to marketing and supply; with Social Enterprise, although this is also the case, it is more than that. The position analysis includes the three triple bottom line values of social wealth, economic viability, and environmental responsibility, as a method to identify the enterprise's relationship with external influences. It does not include the three internal values of common ownership, democracy, and the Social Accounting and Audit system. It does, though, include additional areas such as legal, physical, technical, and political influences.

In the original publication that pioneered Social Enterprise and Social Accounting and Audit, I presented the external view, made up of seven areas where the enterprise can influence external events and where external circumstances can influence the enterprise. This creates an initial context for the enterprise to identify the main influences that affect it, and how it affects the wider environment. These influences can be positive or negative, and can help the enterprise achieve its commercial and non-commercial goals, or hinder it and prevent success. Furthermore, and most importantly, the Position Analysis exercise will help the Audit Team to identify external assumptions being made by the enterprise when planning objectives. Assumptions represent external factors that are outside the enterprise's control, but that the enterprise is dependent on for achieving success. The more the enterprise knows about the assumptions, the easier it will be to exploit the positive elements and mitigate against the negative elements.

The process uses a diagram that is designed to encourage the Audit Team to think about the cost and benefit or strengths and weaknesses of operating in a particular geographical area, and/or servicing or producing within a commercial sector. It sets the scene for more in-depth analysis in determining an enterprise's position vis-a-vis the cost it imposes on society and the environment, and the benefit it generates for society and the ecosystem. It is a simple diagram[15] that leads to questioning how a Social Enterprise can engage more positively in a range of external aspects of society.

Social Accounting and Audit Standards

Social Accounting and Audit Standards are defined as: a systemic, regular, and objective accounting procedure that enables Social Enterprises to establish social, commercial, and environmental criteria, against which they can plan and measure their performance.

To ensure that the results of a Social Accounting and Audit are accurate and trustworthy, there needs to be an agreed quality standard that all Social Enterprises should follow. Compliance with the Social Accounting and Audit Standard assures that certain procedures have been followed and fairness has been applied. All parts of the Social Accounting and Audit Standard should be met for it to be considered as an accurate and fair record of operations. These are:

---

[15] For more details, see Social Audit Toolkit at www.locallivelihoods.com

---

Social Accounting and Audit Standard

1. **Planned and Actual Measurement** – objectives, outcomes, and impact are planned, indicators are set, and results are measured against actual performance. This can be verified through an evidence-based audit trail.
2. **External Stakeholder Involvement** – in light of the six values, external stakeholders, such as customers, suppliers, and local residents, have been actively engaged in the Social Accounting and Audit through online surveys and workshops.
3. **Internal Organisation Assessment** – internal stakeholders, such as co-owners, board members, and volunteers, have been engaged in reviewing the legal and operational structure of the organisation and its commercial operations.
4. **Reporting** – the results shall be presented to co-owners and other stakeholders, and be available online for inspection by the public.
5. **Open Process and Documentation** – the Social Accounting and Audit process and exercises are documented and saved in a manner accessible and understandable to stakeholders, for a minimum of three years.

The Audit Team

The Social Accounting and Audit process needs to be managed in as an objective way as possible. Impartiality is essential, and consequently, the Audit Team must be relatively representative and enthusiastic about exploring truth and reality, and not be swayed by current political relationships or trade policies.

Who should carry out the Social Accounting and Audit process will depend on a number of factors: the size of the enterprise, the complexity of the organisation, and how extensive the process is planned. It is normal to appoint a small team of about three people, preferably including at least one external stakeholder.

At the very start-up stage, co-owners may take on this role, but as the enterprise grows it will be necessary to appoint, on a rotating basis, a smaller group and an external stakeholder as the Audit Team. The Audit Team, as it is known, is responsible for setting the plans, which will be drawn up by management and the Governance Body as part of the annual review and planning. These plans are then integrated into the Social Accounting and Audit system.

Having a balance of internal and external stakeholders gives the results greater credibility. The Governance Body should prepare a Terms of Reference for the Audit Team. The Governance Body then appoints an Audit Team, which will be responsible for carrying out the work and reporting back to stakeholders.

The Audit Team's responsibility includes carrying out the exercises, analysing the results, and identifying new objectives where necessary, a review of staff perceptions, and an assessment of the organisation's impact on the local and broader community. The Audit Team records plans, sets indicators, monitors progress, evaluates, and reports on results. The Audit Team has to set the focus and short-term objectives for the next year, and undertake regular monitoring reports.

Unlike any tick box exercise, Social Accounting and Audit comprises a mixture of planning and measuring indicators and analysed performance, lived experience and observation, open comments, online and face-to-face discussion, and scorecard sliding scale tick boxes.

Social Accounting and Audit Process

This section gives an outline of the Social Accounting and Audit process, and which decisions are taken on how it is carried out. The process is cyclical, it is made up of four incremental elements, and each one follows on from the previous one and informs the next element until the audit circle is completed. The process itself creates a learning culture which grows and strengthens year on year. The four elements of the Social Accounting and Audit process are as follows:

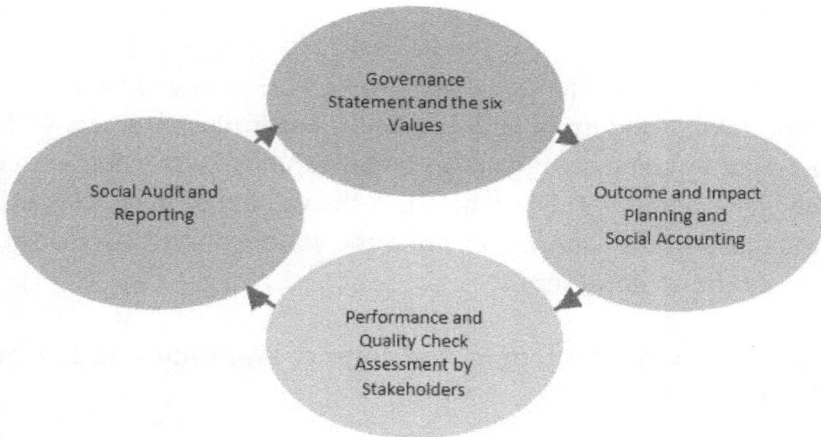

Governance Statement and the six Values

Social Audit and Reporting

Outcome and Impact Planning and Social Accounting

Performance and Quality Check Assessment by Stakeholders

Element One – Governance Statement and the Six Values

Element one is to review and establish clarity about the Social Enterprise: the principles and values, its objectives and commercial operations. Element one starts with a review of the Governance Statement and the six values. The Governance Statement is a written description of the purpose, values, and key objectives of the enterprise. It should be reviewed every audit cycle and, if necessary, updated to reflect the current situation and values. It represents what the Social Enterprise stands for, and provides a valuable framework to guide planning and investment decisions.

Element One includes a review of the constitutional aims and objectives, a review of the rule book, and clarification of the central values that guide the operational management. Value One, 'common ownership' should be reviewed as part of this element to make sure co-owners comprehend their responsibility and the benefits of being an owner. It is also used to represent the Social Enterprise to customers, investors, suppliers, and local communities, and may well be used as part of the commercial marketing.

As part of Element One, the Positioning Analysis is undertaken to identify how the Social Enterprise interacts with external influences, to gain an understanding of the context in which it operates. This will help test the validity of the six values, and position the enterprise within the wider commercial, social, and environmental setting.

Element Two – Outcome and Impact Planning and Social Accounting

Element Two is used to evaluate past plans and plan future objectives and outcomes, and monitor their progress towards impact. Element Two starts with a review of Value Two 'democratic governance' and Value Three 'financial viability'. The process then builds on analysing the critical influences affecting the enterprise, measures the results of the previous plans, and sets new ones for the coming period. The plans will relate to commercial, social, and environmental initiatives that the Social Enterprise decides to invest in. The Governance Body will set the plans, and the Audit Team will fix them within the Social Accounting and Audit system. Also at this point, the Audit Team needs to deepen its analysis of the assumptions the enterprise plans are making and what, if any, mitigating measures can be included.

Accounting and monitoring the plans should be undertaken at least twice a year – once halfway through the year, and again at the end of the year. If required, a Social Enterprise may, of course, monitor plans more regularly.

Element Three – Performance and Quality Check Assessment by Stakeholders

Element Three is used to examine the organisation's performance, and its outcomes and impact (both negative and positive) within its area of influence. Element three includes Value Four 'social wealth creation' and being connected, and Value Five 'environmental responsibility' for living in the natural world. The element comprises stakeholder mapping, profiling, and surveying, and an assessment, by stakeholders, of consistency between the Governance Statement and how they experience interaction with the Social Enterprise.

Stakeholders are co-owners, Governance Body members, customers, suppliers, advisors, volunteers, and local residents, and can be anyone or any other organisation deemed to either influence or be influenced by the Social Enterprise. This will include both an internal and external stakeholder assessment. If the result of the exercise indicates making any changes, these are put to the Governance Body. And if they agree, the Governance Statement is updated.

Scorecard surveying is usually done online, using a simple 4-6 question scorecard survey about the internal and external performance of the enterprise. The questions are related to the Governance Statement, and can be designed to be assessed against the planned targets and behaviour.

Element Four – Social Audit and Reporting

Element Four is when the plans, objectives, and outcomes are analysed and evaluated, and when the stakeholder assessment results are compared to the Governance Statement operations and values. Element four concerns Value Six using the 'Social Accounting and Audit' system of measurement. The previous year's achievements are analysed for their consistency with the Governance Statement to determine the organisation's degree of integrity, and against the planned objectives and assumptions. Objectives that have not been achieved are analysed, the Social Accounting and Audit standards are assessed, and the process and the results are reported formally to stakeholders in the report.

The analysis and audit of the previously planned objectives, outcomes, and overall performance are undertaken at this time, and any plans and objectives still needing to be completed are carried forward. Plans for the next year are prepared, and specific indicators are established for the purpose of monitoring progress.

Reporting is usually annual, although this can be over a more extended period, and will coincide with financial reporting; the two should be presented as a single document. Like a financial audit report, there are standards clauses to be included, and with the Social Accounting and Audit methods, a recommended standard set of clauses and layout structure is provided. The benefit of using standard layout and clauses is that the report becomes easier to read and understand by stakeholders, and guides the reporting to be inclusive and accurate.

Logical Framework

The Logical Framework[16] (Logframe) is an international planning, monitoring, and evaluation tool used in most international development agencies since the mid-1980s. It has gained a reputation for being the most complete and comprehensive tool available. It is undertaken by groups of people or individuals, and prepared on no more than a few pages. As one of the consultants who helped develop and introduce the Logframe method in the programmes and projects supported by the European Union, I have been using it to help structure the commercial, social, and environmental objectives for Social Enterprise, as part of their Social Accounting and Audit system. The particular value of the Logframe is how it combines physical and human behavioural change. Inherent in most social and environmental objectives is the need to change behaviour to utilise the material change. This can often prove more complicated than the physical or technical change, and is often accompanied by identified assumptions. For example, Social Enterprises tend to focus on achieving zero emissions. There first needs to be a positive attitude and a supporting policy towards achieving zero waste and emissions, a behavioural change in the way we manage our energy resources, skills in using new technologies, financial resources to pay for the initial investment, an environmental plan to measure progress towards zero pollution, and ownership to have the authority and power to make positive decisions to change and to see it through to the final result. In the Logframe, both target groups and external assumptions are taken on board and analysed to help design achievable change. The Logframe always helps us understand

---

[16] www.locallivelihoods.com see Social Accounting and Audit Toolkit free download.

the physical and human change required to achieve the objective at the design stage, not after implementation has begun – when it is usually too late.

The Logframe is a matrix with three columns and four rows, which is completed in a particular order. It is particularly useful as a participative tool in enabling groups to be involved in the analysis and design of projects equally. You write brief descriptions in each box and then test the logical relationship between the statements. It is an iterative process, which may require the Audit Team to go through the process several times to get the links right. The benefit of using a matrix is that it's visible and helps groups discuss, and think through, the implications of achieving the objectives. Because it is both a design tool and a management and evaluation tool, the Logframe is used throughout the Social Accounting and Audit process.

Internal Scorecard Organisational Quality Assurance Check

As part of the Social Accounting and Audit Report, the Audit Team should check how the process was undertaken, by using the Quality Assurance Check[17]. You can use numerical scoring or descriptive ones. All co-owners should score the Social Audit Checks individually, and then the Audit Team aggregate the scores into a single score. If the answers are reasonably affirmative, no further action is required; if, however, they are negative, then remedial action might be necessary. These corrective actions should be developed into outline objectives as part of the planning for the next Social Accounting and Audit period. There will be a mix of generic questions and ones associated with a particular enterprise, and it will be the responsibility of the Audit Team to prepare them.

---

[17] www.locallivelihoods.com see Social Accounting and Audit Toolkit free download.

The Triple Bottom Line

The tripartite standards first used in defining a Social Enterprise's core values in 1978 have now become ubiquitous and used in commercial enterprises, State and public bodies, and NGO organisations, often referred to by United Nations' agencies as Profit, People, and Planet. While this level of impact is laudable, there is still a lot of work needed to deepen the practical use of the triple bottom line, to make it more of an integral part of planning, management, and investment.

8.1 Measuring Combined Results

Each of the six values creates a type of wealth and impact in their own right, but when they are combined in the system of a single organisation, the values exponentially create new forms of wealth. The problem with combined wealth is that it is less easy to quantify and measure than, say, financial wealth, and thus difficult to prove. Nonetheless, far from being an impediment, the combined and interlinking six values boost trade, increase learning, and offer alternative and innovative ways to restructure the way many people work.

Common ownership and democracy enhance commitment and responsibility by co-owners to increase productivity and participate in a wider range of activities. Ownership boosts self-esteem, which leads to personal improvement. Democracy is learning to work together and share in decision-making and resource allocation. Empowerment of co-owners through involvement in the organisation will lead to personal improvements, new skills, and work enjoyment. Operating good internal practices will spill over into the local community in which the enterprise is based, and contribute to the wider community wellbeing.

Trade will generate viability and income, and the profits will be used to invest in the enterprise and in purchasing assets for community facilities. Increased productivity and income will increase salaries and also boost tax revenues for the State, and the multiplier effect of local trade will improve the local economy.

Social wealth is gained from people working together and creating more than they can create on their own. A well-functioning Social Enterprise will be empowered to invest in customer service and proper ethical supply chain management. Working together will enable co-owners to invest in environmentally responsible practices, and to support others in also applying new environmental technologies that cut waste and operate zero emission. Environmentally responsible action, integrated into the workplace and in the community, will lower energy and material costs, and enhance biodiversity. To practise what the enterprise advocates will engender customer trust, increase sales, and reduce pollution costs to the State and society.

Combining common ownership and democracy, trade and finance, social and environmentally responsible practices, creates a learning organisation, an enterprise that knows how the future will operate and how the different elements work together in an integrated way. Building integrated organisational systems is part of the strength of Social Enterprise. The combined whole this is part of what a Social Enterprise sells and why customers buy.

The whole worth value is a seventh summative value, a hybrid value. It is dependent on the other six, or any combination of the other values, but not necessarily all of them. Precisely what is meant by whole worth? Is it tangible, is it emotive, is it rooted in a step-up – a form of leverage that results in impact? Partly, the answer lies in a combination of these factors and will, in some cases, be clearly discernible. The whole worth value is likely to be as much about tangible benefits as conscious feelings of wellbeing and happiness. Here are some examples of how whole worth is created and what the impact might be.

Whole worth opens up opportunities for new and, as yet, undefined values. These might be physical, emotional, societal, or natural, and they will be expressed in myriad ways. Whole worth is greater than the sum of the six values, which derives from the energy and insights generated from the interaction and mingling of the mutual benefits created within one organisation. The absence of appropriate measurement values for combined and hybrid benefit doesn't mean the values don't exist. It means they are yet to be adequately formulated with measurable indicators.

Towards zero emissions

There is a need for social attitudes and behaviour to change if we are to achieve zero emissions and the reduction of waste in organisations. There will be a need for extra financial resources to pay for the initial investment; an environmental and business plan, with indicators to know what zero emissions looks like within a particular enterprise; and the ownership and control to have the decision-making power to implement the necessary changes. Combining the planning control, financial investment, and personal and group behaviour, with the eagerness to try and achieve zero emissions and reduced waste, has a chance of success.

Improving the use of technology

A lot of technology, as we know from our computers, is underused. Technology is usually able to perform more tasks than we, the operators, know how to exploit. There is a need to learn new ways of using existing equipment and machinery, apply new technology in innovative ways, and make better use of renewable energy. Personal behaviour needs to change to complement the new technology change; this requires investment in training, and is seen as an essential part of creating alternative organisational systems.

Enabling and improving the way people work together

Through democratic practices, Social Enterprises and their stakeholders will learn better ways to connect, communicate, and make decisions. A Social Enterprise can enlarge the network hub and its range in engaging ever-wider groups of people who are looking to be employed or involved in undertaking work or volunteering. Better use of job sharing, part-time working, and shorter working hours, are just some examples of achieving social wealth benefits.

Reducing the financial cost of utilities and building upkeep

How and what type of building is used to house the enterprise will change as we develop control over planning regulations and building materials. The siting of buildings with south-facing integrated solar panelled roofs must be the first thing to do. The use of renewable energy for lighting, heating, and operating equipment, will naturally follow. The types of materials for furniture, and all the physical materials used to enable people to carry out their work, will need sourcing carefully. Reducing the cost of utilities will regenerate the environment.

Inspiring happiness and self-awareness

Having a sense of integrity – acting in unison with one's belief systems as well feeling that our actual situation corresponds closely to ambitions – is a measure of happiness. In inclusive environments, greater opportunities exist for individuals to access resources and support in developing innovative human and technical change. Trust and empathy will underpin new and innovative initiatives based on sharing and democracy; opening opportunities for the enterprise and the local community to work together in extending the impact of shared initiatives.

Being part of the local community will enable stakeholders to come forward with ideas that, together, the enterprise and community can develop, to create new work opportunities and local enterprises.

Spreading the wealth widely

To achieve whole worth, the impact of outcomes would naturally spread beyond the confines of the enterprise, and be experienced more widely in the community and beyond. To achieve impact requires time and the broader participation of stakeholders. There is always the need to provide and support as well as change human behaviour and utilise what's on offer.

Exactly how and what type of whole worth will be created out of the combined six elements is difficult to predict. Starting with simple and, in many ways, apparent connections, as previously described – through feedback loops and the emergence of more complex connections – new and at times unforeseen benefits will ensure. These are likely to be experienced as humanist and emotional gratification, as well as technological outcomes.

Organisations that adopt and combine the six values will thrive in the 21st century, as they will attract investment, customers, and trading partners. And those that do not will wither.

Social Enterprise is setting the trend for the next millennium in how organisations are structured. In the interconnected world of the 21st century, Social Enterprise is setting modern principles by which trade should be governed in the future.

9 OWNERSHIP IS ECONOMICS

Ownership and economics are inextricably tied together: who owns, controls; and who controls gets the wealth and power, runs the economy, and has an undue societal influence. We are currently confronting two parallel economic problems: ownership and financial inequality. Too many fixed assets are owned by too few people, and obsessive reliance on GDP and profit maximisation as the sole indicator of success or failure. Both need radical change.

Surplus value (profit) used to be thought of as that produced by labour. During the 18th and 19th centuries, many thinkers speculated on the composition of surplus value, from where and how did it derive? Marx, among others, argued that labour is only a part of the input to produce the good or service, and that 'nature is just as much a source of use values'. Since then, of course, monetarist theory has gained ascendency, to the extent that unorganised labour in terms of things like the gig economy has no inherent value other than time spent working for the hourly wage. But with the triple bottom line, recognition of the other inputs to produce the surplus values has broadened to include financial (capital), society (family, skills, education, community, and labour), and nature (water, air, untilled soil, minerals, and landscape). Nature is referred to in old economics as 'constant capital'. The owners of these three inputs are therefore due their cut of the surplus value. In Social Enterprise, the owners of capital and labour are the same, and the owners of the environment are society. That is why some of the surplus value is invested in reducing raw material use, reusing materials, and recycling material waste to be reused. If we accept that the triple bottom indices represent the primary inputs of surplus value, then it follows that all three must share the rewards.

Social Enterprise is part of the engine room of the economy. Like private enterprise, it buys and sells goods and services and, in the process, creates surplus value. Surplus value is the profit an enterprise makes from trading. Whoever owns the company owns the profit, and decides how that is spent. The difference between private business and Social Enterprise is in who owns the enterprise and how they choose to spend the profits.

The economic system derives from private ownership, by the State and individuals. Their common thread is that this system puts control and decision-making in the hands of a very few people, who use their position to appropriate surplus value. Through globalisation of law and commerce and the use of the internet to manage transactions, the surplus value has grown and accumulated in such huge, concentrated piles, so that today, we have a situation where 1% of the population owns over 50% of all global assets. The degree of polarisation between the 1% and the 99% of people who share the rest is inherently dangerous – it cannot be left to the 1% to decide the future. The 1% asset-owning population cannot reconcile the diametrically opposing criteria of performance of the interests of the elites and the interests of society, simply because asset ownership is not only a legal right and power; it is also a sense of worth and a sense of self-esteem. Without a fundamental change to asset ownership, there will be no change to mass inequality. The polarisation is set on a course to continue and worsen; there is nothing to stop the 1% from grabbing more and more, so leaving the other 99% with less and less. We operate an ownership and economic system that is designed for infinite resources, land, buildings, water, and minerals, whereas, in reality, they are finite and limited. Only since the 20th century has society recognised the limits to growth of a finite planet and an ever-expanding human population. The overpopulation of planet earth and the global neoliberal economy's dash for private ownership has precipitated the squeeze on resources, and that has led to the present levels of inequality we now experience. To state the obvious, overuse of resources and land on a finite planet and the continuous dash for growth are incompatible, and at worst they are in conflict, as is overpopulation and limited resources.

There is the classic and, in its day, revolutionary idea of Adam Smith's notion of trade and accumulation of wealth being good, not only for the owners such as the baker, but also for the baker's assistant. The more bread the baker sells, the more assistants get jobs, and the more jobs created, the more bread is bought, and so on. Primarily, the economic system is based on the 'free market' where goods and services are freely traded and priced according to the buyers' and sellers' mutual agreement. Economics based on scarcity and supply and demand might well confirm Smith's thesis of trickledown economics. Strangely, China's recent economic growth attests to that thesis. In the world of automation and post-scarcity, where 'supply and marketing' – and not 'supply and demand' – is the dominant economic model, growth has no limits. Without the natural limit of supply, growth becomes dangerous. Greed dominates growth, and growth in a digital age, based on supply and marketing, is limitless. Limitless growth dominated by greed exploits labour and the environment equally. This outdated concept of 'growth is good' makes financial wealth for the few owners of assets and, consequently, loses financial, social, and environmental wealth for the many.

Growth

Our classical economic models, whether Keynesian, monetarism, or State-controlled, all aspire to growth as the engine of the economy. Growth in terms of turnover and profit is simple, clear, and measurable as a goal; it dominates economic action and occupies the place of God in economic thinking. It is the common purpose of all those involved in the economy, and is measured in terms of how much money you have. The other problem with growth is that it is nearly always associated with 'something good', to grow physically, mentally, spiritually, or socially, are aspirational and seen as beyond reproach.

Growth has been so successful that we are now overgrown, and are reaching the limits to growth predicted over 40 years ago. If growth continues on the same trajectory, we are likely to burn ourselves to death and destroy most of the habitat on the planet. The wealthy people who influence this approach, of course, have resources to move off-planet and settle on a 'space yacht'. But the rest of us are likely to burn or drown in the slipstream of economic growth.

Growth at the current level of the world population, the natural resource extraction, industrial processing, and consumption that the planet is experiencing, is not sustainable. The fact that the many poor people on the earth need more, and the few rich people need less, is not a moral or political dilemma any more; it has become a survival issue. The present economic growth models are also caught in an economic bind of their own making, and have, for this reason alone, become untenable. The models based on growth need to expand continuously, and to do that they need to borrow ever more amounts of money. The guarantee of repayment for this borrowing, mountains of corporate debt, is predicated on forecasts of growth and the eventual actual growth. We experience an economic system trapped in a cycle of debt-growth-repayment-more debt, which we might call the 'cycle of economic, societal, and environmental erosion'. Under the present system, when the debt is greater than the ability to repay, the borrowing entity relinquish power and become indebted to the lender. Whether the borrowing entity is an individual, company, region, or nation, it supports the accumulation of wealth in fewer hands.

How to move away from the ravages of growth is going to be difficult. We need to be aware why we should, and it's because the planet we live on can't take any more denuding of the biosphere and then re-covering the earth with waste. We are beginning to understand and accept that there is a need to adopt attitudes and policies to start reducing growth and waste in equal measure. Being materially frugal individually and in the family and company is the next step. Once there is a critical mass of material frugality, society then starts to change, and the planet breathes new life.

To pull back from the headlong dive into the cycle of erosion, Social Enterprise facilitates two counterweights. Through the common ownership system, growth becomes less urgent than securing good quality and viable income. And, secondly, the regenerative policy and approaches adopted by Social Enterprise mean that they don't grow their business by manufacturing throwaway items; they tend to focus on products and services with long life and reusable qualities.

Ownership of assets

Ownership is history itself; it defines the nature of history, and tells a story of society reaching back well over 13000 years, when Neolithic farmers started to bury their dead family members in elaborate graves to 'mark their territory' and stake their claim over the ownership of the land they cared for and which gave them food and sustenance. Ownership is our heritage, and defines how we and others see us and our relationship to other people and other bodies. To roll back inequality and spread fairness, shared ownership is essential.

Owning assets, land, buildings, machinery, patent rights, is less about money and more about control and decision-making. If you own assets, you pay no rent and have more money; if you own buildings and machinery, you control how they are used; if you own land, you control what is done on it, and how that affects the environment; and, if you own patent rights, you control the use of its intellectual outputs, and receive regular income.

We are in the throes of an automation revolution, where a few people own most assets, many people have jobs, income, and limited assets, and increasing numbers have no secure jobs and no assets. Economists call this 'hollowing out', where there will likely be jobs at the high-end managing assets, and at the low end of the skills' chain where it will be cheaper to employ cleaners than buy a robot. But in the middle, it is forecast, AI-powered automation will be applied, and many paying jobs lost. As yet, there is little or no discussion on how automation is likely to pan out, and no debate about how employees will be displaced and in what manner. The present Coronavirus pandemic hastens the move towards AI-automation, without a question of consequence, based on the fallacious urgency to 'get the economy moving again'. If is likely, that the pandemic is not a one-off, but a new normal in some shape or form, we can't pretend that anything is the same and that we just get 'moving again'. The pandemic is a disaster, and also an opportunity, though there is no evidence that the 1% see it that way. Instead, they will want to get back to pre-pandemic growth economics, as though the pandemic is an aberration.

Just take one industry that employs, in every country, millions of people: food. The process of supplying food is being automated at breakneck speed. Intensive livestock rearing and greenhouse-managed food production are largely automated. Conveyor belts controlled by barcoded instructions already provide warehousing and packaging, and automated supermarket shelf-stacking and checkouts are being rolled out. We are witnessing the bits of the supply chain being linked by self-driving lorries. Soon, once home delivery is more common, there will be no need for the supermarkets at all; delivery will be from warehouse to home. This is no secret; it is happening now in front of us, in full view. The millions of lost jobs and incomes will strain the economy, as we have no idea how people will earn a living. If they own no assets, and robots have replaced their labour, what then?

The essential change Social Enterprise makes is not so much with the business viability, not the social care bestowed on staff and community, and not the responsible environmental behaviour. It is the ownership of the assets by the many co-owners, and their ability to influence and shape their communities that matters most. There is nothing to stop people owning their own business other than themselves. The legal right is well established, finance is available, and there are many suppliers and customers ready to trade. It is a personal attitude and the unpreparedness to put effort into taking responsibility and doing it, that matters most.

Social Enterprise is predicated on common ownership and the control of surplus value. There is no way more effective in achieving this change than in using the rule of law to change the way business is owned. As we know 'ownership is nine-tenths of the law'. If anyone wants to create social benefit, there is no more immediate, easy, and sustainable way than to establish common ownership over the enterprise by the people who create the wealth.

Owners of Social Enterprise are workers, communities, customers, and partners, thus broadening asset ownership to more people, securing income and assets for them and their communities. Social Enterprise improves the microeconomic conditions of co-owners and their families and the enterprise's local community. Ownership of assets is a prerequisite to control and decision-making. It is an indispensable requirement for change – there will be no change unless and until there is a change of asset ownership and control. And, even if the working process is automated, co-owners still own the assets and will receive dividends as a share of their ownership.

Incentives

In recent times, both the State-run and neoliberal economic systems have suffered near collapse due, in no small part, to the influence of incentives. In our time, we have witnessed the complete bankruptcy of the Soviet Union (1990), and the near collapse of the neoliberal economics of the capitalist West (2008). False claims of success and abundance heralded the collapse of both these economic systems. In the Soviet Union, the outputs of the five-year plans were never real; they showed an increase on the year before, knowingly pretending towards growth and then falsified the results, while at the same time the retail outlets had empty shelves and scarcity of essential goods. This was plain to see after the collapse of the Soviet Union in the early 1990s, when I worked in the 15 former Soviet Union countries. In the West, the bankers' greed got the better of them, and they created subprime housing stock that was worthless in real money. These unscrupulous bankers had mixed and matched worthless stock with good value stock. The difference was hidden in the packaged export of selling the mixed debt to other, unscrupulous, bankers in other countries. And as the banks defaulted and closed their doors, Western citizens saw the value of their currency nosedive and austerity kick in.

The incentives used to keep the economies on track failed. In the former Soviet Union, the absolute lack of financial incentives meant that it was easier for people not to bother to work hard or invest their mental and physical abilities to be in any way creative or entrepreneurial. The lesson learned was clear; goodwill by citizens towards an ideology will only last so long, and goodwill eventually dies. There was just no incentive for people to get up in the morning and go to work. Conversely, in the West, the opposite was the case. The incentive for bankers to legally mix and match dud stock with good stock, and sell packaged goods to other bankers, was spurred on by the lure of colossal bonuses. The incentives were too great, and corrupted bankers' ability to manage their funds decently and legally. Because the incentives were so big – unlike those in the former Soviet Union economy – they didn't even go to bed, and were already at their desks before daybreak. Incentives need proportionality, neither too much, nor too little, but just right. I do think incentives are useful; they not only help when motivating people to do that extra bit of hard work needed by the enterprise, but they help individuals achieve their goal for additional money for a specific purpose.

Incentive in Social Enterprise is often frowned upon. I think that is because it is seen as an extravagance and can lead to excessive exploitation. My view is that bonuses and incentives in general can be creative and rewarding of hard work and innovation. Used in a proportionate way, bonus as a percentage of net profit is recognition of co-owners' efforts, and should be part of the internal decision-making for profit disbursement at the end of each year. Other incentives based on innovation or meeting a delivery target may also earn a small sum. Incentives, also, don't need to always be in the form of money; they can be extra holiday time, working only half days, bringing cared-for children to work, etc.

Economics for Social Enterprise

At the heart of Social Enterprise is a regenerative approach, where the emphasis is not on getting bigger and making more, but on growing the idea and practice of regenerative sustainability. Humanity is supported by working and trading, socialising between individuals, and by reliance on nature and the biosphere for wellbeing and stability. The present system of growth is unsustainable, and the current state of the biosphere is untenable. Therefore, we have nothing to sustain, and we need to adopt a regenerative and not a sustainability approach. Social Enterprise uses a regenerative system through the interrelationships of the six values – each one is a standalone value and, at the same time, part of the combined regenerative value. The complementary nature of the values grows the mutual beneficial interrelationship between them, and checks any negative impact that any one value may impose. It has never been about 'social' or 'environmental' or 'ownership'; it is the interrelationship that counts, which is where the learning and change take place, and where the benefit to society and the planet as a whole, emanates.

Today, the circular economy is the new economic system which is forcing many large corporations into considering the environmental consequences of their operations. The circular economy is driven by the need for regenerative systems to cut waste and pollution, and instigate closed-loop approaches to manufacturing and agriculture through the design of processes and materials that repair, reuse, and recycle material resources. It is an alternative to the traditional linear economic approach focused on growth and exploitation of human and natural resources.

The circular economic approach can be applied to organisational development as well as physical manufacturing and supply chain management. We have seen this gradual shift since Kenneth Boulding, in 1966,[18] raised awareness of the

---

[18] Kenneth Boulding was an English economist and in 1966 wrote a book entitled *The Economics of the Coming Spaceship Earth*

unsustainable nature of the open economy, based on the use and disposal of resources, and suggested that this should be replaced by a closed-loop economic system whereby reuse and recycling became the dominant approach. Kate Raworth further extended this closed-looped approach in her excellent book, *Doughnut Economics*, where she promotes the need for a new economic model and the need for '21st-century economists'. The circular economy model deals directly with the environmental issues of waste and pollution through its regenerative design concepts, but it doesn't tackle the problems of ownership and inequality directly.

At the microeconomic level, Social Enterprise, by following the definition of the six values, will retain surpluses and invest them locally in the enterprise, community, and local assets. Local asset ownership will provide resources and facilities accessible to local people to share. These might have to be paid for, or they may be used free of charge, but in any event, the opportunity to share resources through common ownership reduces the need to buy so much, and broadens out the use-value of the assets for those who cannot afford to purchase the items individually.

Here is one example out of hundreds. There is a case for each household to buy an electric hairdryer that is used daily, but there is no need for each home to buy an electric drill that is often only used a few times a year. There is excellent scope to reduce purchases of rarely used items, as long as residents learn to commonly own and share responsibility for the items as if they were solely owned. Sharing is seen by some as the antithesis of trade, but commonly-owned assets are there to be shared. One of the aims of Social Enterprise is to support the common accumulation of assets for sharing. The economics of sharing is financially efficient and at several levels, socially rewarding and environmentally responsible.

The economics of shared resource utilisation is inexpensive to operate and administer. Admittedly, users of shared resources have to learn to take responsibility for items that are not theirs. Although this is often cited as the reason why sharing doesn't work, it is, however, the experience of Social Enterprises that proves this wrong. Sharing finite resources, whether natural or manufactured, is going to become increasingly more urgent. This is where Social Enterprise has a role, from its experiences of sharing ownership, management, assets, and resources, and in developing innovative ways for human behaviour that leads to the efficient management of the process of sharing. Learning to be responsible for shared resources and facilities with people you don't know is going to become a significant challenge for the new economics. Shared assets and resources are part of the value-added regenerative economics.

The notion of community economy within national and international economies is entirely realistic once Social Enterprise becomes a more widely used form of business organisation. Using surpluses for local investment, rather than using them to be sequestered away to shareholders, would significantly enhance the community economy. A community economy, though, doesn't exist in isolation. It is part of a broader economy, but because it retains wealth that would otherwise be lost, it bolsters local trade and commerce, leading to the multiplier effect of a circular economy. It supports new ventures, employment, and local asset accumulation.

Circular local economics can also withstand the detrimental effect of national and international boom-and-bust economic cycles, where typically the result is more acutely felt in local communities by poorer sections of society. Poor people have different priorities to those who manage the economy, and have no say in the decisions made. The cause of the boom-and-bust cycles is rarely a financial breakdown; it is due to political posturing, and disputes, and human greed, anywhere in the world. Social Enterprise, with its emphasis on wider profit distribution, makes it possible for local economies, everywhere in the world, to become stronger and more self-determining, which will increase the resilience of communities to widen their control and offset economic fluctuations in the national and international economies.

'Reclaim Our Locality' should become our slogan. We can operate locally, we can own our land, buildings, and assets locally, and we can create simple democratic systems of governance over them. Social Enterprise is uniquely structured for such tasks; it has the legal framework, democratic governance, and the modern principles of profit, people, and planet performance measurement, not to mention a 40-year track record.

It's already happening. Local groups are springing up, preventing bad development and supporting proper development, in the form of reclaiming bankrupt pubs, libraries, shops, care services, child services, transport, agriculture, manufacturing, and retail. These initiatives to recover our locality work, because they are driven by local people who have vested interests in providing the product/service and varying degrees of time and expertise. Building a new form of economy based on straightforward and local transactions, building a locally owned asset base and technology platforms, are ours for the doing.

Social Enterprises are stepping up to the challenge of reclaiming our locality and countering the overwhelming influence of the technology and financial monopolies. Not that globalisation is going away, but a more balanced society where globalisation and local communities operate in parallel would, I suggest, be a much better option than the current emphasis on globalisation or nothing. Localities, of course, will only in the long term challenge the monopolies, but our concern is with creating local circular economies for the residents of local communities. Putting more people in control of their lives will trickle up to responsible global connections, trade, and social behaviour. It is an unfair trade when, in reality, only a tiny bit of economic benefit trickles down, but a whole lot of intellectual and innovative ideas trickle up, usually free of charge.

The economics of Social Enterprise is not dissimilar from the economics of any business, which is why they are technically easy to set up and run. They trade competitively, borrow finance, pay salaries, produce goods and services, sell them at a profit, and are subject to the same statutory and fiscal regimes. Social Enterprise operates in the market place and pays taxes like any business, anywhere in the world. Because there are no external shareholders, all profits are invested in five ways: first, in terms of salaries and bonuses to co-owners; second, as re-investment in the commercial operations; third, as donations to achieve its social and environmental objectives; fourth, as a contribution to the reserve fund; and fifth, as national and local taxes. Unlike other businesses where dividends are paid to shareholders – both individual and corporate, wherever they reside – Social Enterprises distribute their financial wealth locally through high salaries to staff and for social and environmental objectives, most often local. Surplus value traditionally trickles up as dividends paid to shareholders. In our case, profits trickle sideways to the surrounding local economy, which then multiplies as it circulates locally, enhancing the general wellbeing of communities.

As Marx defined it, surplus value is the difference between the cost of production and the selling price of the goods. This is an inherent value created by workers, investors, and managers, converting inputs into outputs. In contrast, the added value from a

Social Enterprise is an external value created by using the internal surplus value to pay for the social and environmental investments, instead of shareholders appropriating the profits in the form of dividends. The surplus value generated by Social Enterprise is the same as that created by private corporations; the difference lies in the use value of surplus. In private business, it is used for commercial re-investment and as dividends for shareholders. In contrast, in Social Enterprise, it is used for commercial re-investment and social and environmental good practice investment. The external investment of the internal surplus value contributes to society and the planet. Over time, this should enable Social Enterprise to reduce tax payments to the State as a percentage of the amount invested in non-returnable investments for the enterprise – investments in external social and environmental initiatives usually paid for by the State out of tax receipts.

The broader distribution of financial wealth to individuals and communities is the main change the economics of Social Enterprises brings. Over time, this will impact on the balance of wealth in the world. All the wealth that would typically flow to already wealthy shareholders, who often spend it on luxury items in far-off lands, will stay local through the multiplier effect of the circular economy.

Raising investment finance in most cases is the same as for private business; one crucial difference is that Social Enterprise is ineligible to use the national Stock Market to raise funds. They don't issue voting shares, but they can provide debenture stock (a type of preferential loan stock that makes fixed payments at scheduled intervals of time, but carries no voting rights). The recent innovation in online crowdfunding, impact investments, community investment, and revolving loan funds, means that Social Enterprise has access to a wide range of financial instruments from which to raise finance. As they grow, and the demand for financial services also grows, further innovation in financial mechanisms will be developed. For example, the current research being undertaken in the UK, into designing a Social Enterprise Stock Market, is an important step in that direction, but still needs many more such initiatives.

Individual intellectual property rights over innovative products will need a different type of contract. In the private sector, the inventor of a product will hold most of the shares in the company, guaranteeing the control and profits. This is handled differently to attract inventors of products to set up or work in Social Enterprise. Instead of holding a majority share, they would be given contractual licences for their invention, being paid a licence fee for every item sold. They would, therefore, be paid their salary, and also a fee for their invention. As the demand for this type of arrangement grows, we can expect further innovation in the legal provision and patent payment systems.

Recruiting co-owners is as competitive for Social Enterprise as it is for private enterprise; the benefit of the former is that, in addition to salaries, co-owners will also receive bonuses as a dividend on their ownership stake. Salaries tend to be on the high side for the sectors, and the differential between the lowest and highest paid staff is narrower than similar sector companies. Most Social Enterprises practise a 3-to-1 maximum differential pay scale policy. Some Social Enterprises practise parity salaries, with every worker receiving the same hourly rate regardless of their position; in such cases, investment in training and job rotations is prioritised. Not only are there greater opportunities for work interest and skill acquisition, but job satisfaction increases substantially, and staff retention is consequently improved.

The contribution Social Enterprise makes in skill training, better salaries, recruitment policy, environmental clean-up, and social service welfare costs to those discriminated against, is considerable, and will one day be calculated and ideally be tax-deductible as a non-returnable investment.

Government Policy

To develop a fiscal and monetary policy to support Social Enterprise, there first needs to be a legally agreed definition. It is necessary to formulate a Social Enterprise Act with a set of model rules as the formal basis for developing a proper set of mechanisms and policies to enable the sector to spread. National Accounting Regulatory Bodies will need to formulate social and environmental accounting procedures that are acceptable to them and Revenue authorities. This again will need a government edict to give authority to the Revenue authorities and accounting regulatory bodies to instigate the development of the procedures and auditing checks.

Up to this point, there is limited government support for Social Enterprise. In the UK, for example, the Community Interest Company Act 2004 (CIC) is the one policy initiative that the UK government supported, and it, as it turns out, is not to do with Social Enterprise but with community organisations having an asset lock imposed on their assets. The European Union has supported the introduction of a 'social procurement' clause, where public bodies are obliged to include social and environmental criteria when assessing and awarding contracts. But, as research has shown[19], this clause cannot be implemented unless and until Social Enterprise is legally defined. If and when Social Enterprise is defined, and such a social procurement clause is instigated, the benefit of having all public contracts

---

[19] EU research

aligned with social and environmental good practice would be very welcome.

Social Enterprise will need different types of financial investment, such as monetary policy on interest rates to create favourable conditions for Social Enterprise would be extremely beneficial. Appropriate fiscal policy, for example, could be corporation tax relief on investment for internal training, to enable co-owners to learn about management and planning, and the introduction of innovative technologies to use, reuse, and recycle waste materials.

Both monetary and fiscal policy can only be formulated once Social Enterprise is defined by an Act of Parliament, with the requisite model rules and Accounting Regulatory Body's endorsement of the Social Accounting and Audit system. To enact a legal and registered Social Enterprise will require pulling together a number of strands to include an agreed Social Enterprise definition:

- a Social Enterprise Act
- a set of model rules as the legal constitutional charter for registration
- a government authority authorised to register Social Enterprise; the National Accounting Regulatory Bodies authorised to create a Social Accounting and Audit procedure and regulation, to include social wealth accounting and reporting, and environmental assessment accounting and reporting
- the formation of a Social Enterprise Oversight Board to coordinate and quality assure the process of formulating the Social Enterprise regulatory functions of government

10 BEING LEGAL IS BEING POWERFUL

Up to this point, if you want to form a Social Enterprise, just about anywhere in the world, you will have to use a legal structure not specifically designed for the purpose. There are no model rules for a constitutional charter with the requirements of the six values and the Social Accounting and Audit system, or a legislative act passed by any country's government to support Social Enterprise. There is also no legal form of the triple bottom line that I am aware of, or any attempt to formulate such specifications for business or non-government organisations. Yet, there are hundreds of thousands of legally registered organisations calling themselves Social Enterprise. In the UK, the model rule formed by the 1976 Industrial Common Ownership Act is still the main charter Social Enterprises use to register their company. In many other countries, they use an array of different types of charter, and customise them as far as possible.

The process of developing the Industrial Common Ownership Act 1976 was not complicated; it just needed the political will of the then government of the day, and support from lawyers interested enough to draft the Act. The result of passing the ICO Act had a tremendous effect. It facilitated the development of many groups to form registered worker cooperatives for their commercial ventures. The model rules, with minor amendments, are still being used to this day. Although ICOM no longer exists, the model rules were taken over by Co-op UK (the main body of the cooperative societies in the UK), which continues to support start-up worker cooperatives.

To formulate model rules and get an Act of Government passed, needs political will by elected politicians. However, before they can submit a draft Act for consideration, politicians need to have a clear definition on which to base the draft Act. They will not and should not be the people to draft the definition. As we have seen, there is no accepted Social Enterprise definition, and until there is one, politicians will not be able to support enacting legislation. There is no technical reason why there shouldn't be a purposely designed statutory Social Enterprise Act and accompanying model rule charter, which includes the common ownership and democratic governance, has the three operational triple bottom line aims, and the requirement to undertake Social Accounting and Audit.

A Social Enterprise must be legally registered to secure the rights and fair shares for co-owners and controllers of their place of work. Without a legally registered constitutional charter, Social Enterprise is just a term with no meaning. Sometimes companies call themselves a Social Enterprise, but are owned and controlled by an individual or by a holding company. These are not Social Enterprises. They may be working for the right causes of a social or environmental mission, and may even work collectively. Just giving a percentage of net profits to charity and calling it a social mission enterprise is not enough; it is incidental to Social Enterprise. They are often dependent on an individual or shareholders' goodwill. History has shown that goodwill only lasts as long as everything is going well. In the event of a downturn, or opportunity for other types of trading or technical problems, the goodwill is overridden and the legal owner steps in and takes control.

Having thousands of operating Social Enterprises around the world, and no clear and universal definition, and no specific legal charter, you would think sounds contradictory. But that is precisely what is happening. However, as long as the joint-stock company system legislation exists, Social Enterprise can exist. But it is the case that when setting up and registering Social Enterprise using a joint stock company act, groups have to adopt an inappropriate legal charter to register their enterprise. The rights and responsibilities of shareholders is radically changed from those who invest capital to those who invest labour.

In some countries, such as the UK, there is a range of legal charters which can be adapted and designed for Social Enterprises and cooperatives; in other countries, there is no specific constitutional charter available. However, there is usually some form of legal charter that can be amended to provide a structure for Social Enterprises. The Joint Stock Company, the Co-op Act, or a registered Association, is available in most countries, and they can be adapted to register a Social Enterprise. Any form of Joint Stock Company, for example, in just about any country, can be legally formulated to include the six Social Enterprise values within the legal charter.

Having to adapt to existing legal charters is, however, very unsatisfactory. The main reason for this is that when groups or lawyers change existing charters without the six values and the Social Accounting and Audit procedure, they formulate weak clauses about ownership and democracy. Also, they are unable to align the requirement to include a Social Accounting and Audit system with both existing company law and the accounting practice code of conduct in the country. Other reasons are that if there is insufficient legal advice, the wording of constitutional clauses is oversimplified, 'dumbed down', leading to problems if the enterprise becomes engaged in a legal dispute or is challenged in any way. A test of any good charter is its ability to withstand legal challenges.

A charter is made up of two documents: the first is the Memorandum of Association, and the second is the Articles of Association. The memorandum explains the purpose and objectives of the enterprise, and the articles describe how the enterprise is owned, structured, and governed.

The Memorandum of Association (the purpose and objectives) has some standard clauses about the purpose. These are general clauses stipulating the main commercial purpose of the enterprise, and are designed to be adapted for each enterprise to write their objectives. For a Social Enterprise, the purpose and objectives will include commercial trading aims, social wealth and wellbeing, and environmental objectives and responsibility. Within the charter, these clauses are always written specifically for particular enterprises. For example, a Social Enterprise that uses Social Accounting and Audit, in addition to the financial audit, will have to add the intention to conduct a Social Accounting and Audit and briefly describe the process. This will be needed in both the Memorandum of Association and in the Articles of Association, and if not well drafted, can lead to legal disputes with stakeholders.

In the Articles of Association (the organisational structure and management system), there will mostly be statutory clauses, but critically, the clauses on membership, voting rights, the structure of management, and the shareholder value, will be amendable. So even if there is no specific legal charter suitable in a particular country, it is very likely that a standard joint stock company structure can be amended to create the framework for registration. The key difference is that workers are members, and members are shareholders, and each member only has one vote, and all co-owners are registered as directors. There are some forms of Social Enterprise where shares are distributed in unequal numbers, but still each member, regardless of the number of shares, only has one vote. For example, workers can accrue financial shares based on the length of service. On leaving, the co-owners can sell their shares back to the enterprise and collect a fair share of their labour inputs. Furthermore, Social Enterprises sometimes use what is known as an 'asset lock'. An asset lock is a legal stipulation that, in the event of the enterprise being wound up or closing down for whatever reason, any remaining assets – after all debts have been paid – shall be disbursed to a named charitable organisation. This, of course, means that co-owners will not be entitled to any of the assets that remain. An asset lock is very suitable for community enterprises that have received, in whatever form, public funds and/or assets from public bodies or charities. For example, if a community social enterprise has been given a redundant building by a local government body (a public body), it would be appropriate for it to be returned to public ownership in the event of the enterprise closing down.

During the 1970s in the UK, a few radical organisations enacted a voluntary 'asset lock' in their constitution, whereby, in the event of the organisation being wound up and closed down, the assets would automatically be transferred to another named organisation. Based on this experience, in 2005, the UK Government formulated a new company regulation called The Community Interest Company Regulation (CIC) 2005. The regulation established the Asset Lock that meant on dissolution all remaining assets would be transferred to a nominated charitable organisation. The Asset Lock provision is beneficial when setting up community-owned organisations or organisations that are less commercial than a sole trading company. But for many Social Enterprises which are solely trading, the Asset Lock may well be a hindrance when attempting to raise finance, either investment or a loan, because it may compromise the investment or loan guarantee repayment potential.

A fuller description of how to conduct the Social Accounting and Audit system will need to be included in the Articles of Association. The design of the system will need aligning with the specific country's National Accounting Regulatory Body's professions code of conduct. This is necessary because the Accounting Regulatory codes will most probably not include social and environmental accounting. In the future, and especially if the Social Enterprise Act has been passed, a charter will only have to refer to the accounting code, as with financial auditing, which will include the fuller description of the standards and criteria that must be followed.

Should we have a special Social Enterprise charter and a supporting legislative Act?

We have always had a Social Enterprise definition – one defined in the 1981 publication 'Social Audit – A Management Tool for Co-operative Working' and subsequent 'Social Enterprise Planning Toolkit', where the definition has remained more or less the same for over 40 years, with minor clarifications in the different editions of the publications. But as we have seen in Chapter 6, many organisations choose to water down the definition to appeal to a wider audience.

We have a Social Enterprise definition, we have sufficient and robust clauses for the use of Social Accounting and Audit, and we have the basic template to guide groups in preparing their purpose and objectives, their organisation structure, and the ownership and control governance system. What we don't have is the Act of Parliament (government) to enshrine a legislative set of module rules specifically for Social Enterprise. Though there is no international mechanism for introducing legislation to incorporate corporate structures, most countries recognise each other's business registration systems, and will accept a legal structure from a European country, such as the UK.

In the past, I have said that we should participate voluntarily to prevent the State from getting too involved. This is because I have always expected that if they were involved, they would do it badly, put people off, and then when the next election comes around the business lobby would try to revoke the legislation. And instead of the tripartite values being central to organisations' core objectives, they would then become something to get around and subvert. Nevertheless, I now think it is time to pass in law a Social Enterprise Act and not to rely on voluntary structures, as experience shows this leads to watering down the definition and enfeebling the essence of Social Enterprise.

In my opinion, the absence of a Social Enterprise Act and accompanying model rule has held back the development of Social Enterprise around the world. Social Enterprise is the right structure to counterbalance the excessively negative impact of global capitalism, and share the rewards of all our labour more equally and fairly. If there were an internationally recognised Social Enterprise definition, and a legal and organisational structure able to be registered in all countries, using existing legislation and intentional module rules, the growth of Social Enterprises would accelerate significantly.

The government often provides supporting funds when passing Acts, to help implement the new legal structure. This is usually not very much, but enough to get the Act and accompanying supportive rules integrated into mainstream systems, specifically, informing the legal profession of the new Act, including the Act and accompanying model rules in Business Schools and other educational institutions, and providing the legal and organisational foundation for support agencies involved in developing new Social Enterprises.

The need for a Social Enterprise Act and model rules is overwhelming; the economic fallout from the global pandemic is only just being understood. For many millions of people around the world, the fallout will be catastrophic. There will be a proportion of people who will significantly benefit from forming Social Enterprises to own and manage local resources and productive processes for their local communities. People with the greatest need will not have the wherewithal or time to invest in formulating legal charters. A Social Enterprise Act and model rules would greatly facilitate their ability to form and set up appropriate legal structures to help establish local resources for survival and long-term prosperity.

11 REFLECTION AND RENEWAL

So, what's to be done? The world is burning with fire, floods, pestilence, loss of biodiversity, and extreme inequalities; people are enraged, in their hundreds of thousands, and taking to the streets around the world in major cities and industrial sites to voice their anger. Even more people are fleeing their homes and countries in search of survival. Politicians tell us these are local problems; corporate CEOs let it be known that it's not their concern; and the media exploits the turmoil by splashing alarmist headlines across their front pages. I know the rage is the result of inequality, in terms of having no voice, not having a fair share of the globe's finite survival resources, and still being beholden to old-fashioned delusional mythologies of gods, sermons, and devils. There is still, after all we know, only the UN's Universal Declaration of Human Rights that stands for a pragmatic global ethical code.

The rage is universal and sparked by the cupidity of politicians, corporate leaders, and the military, being footloose with the essence of human rights. The causes are an economic system fated to favour the rich at the expense of the poor. And a climate catastrophe that is out of control and ignored by the rich, whose industries cause the pollutants, and who, if they ceased polluting, would likely stop being so rich. The catch-22 nightmare we're in is caused by the structural system we create. In the past, wars and violent insurrection were the result of similar rages, and we have learned from those historical experiences that we are rightly hesitant in going down that road. We have the respect and enforcement of the law, democracy, and communication, to change the structural system by peaceful means. What seems to be lacking is the physiological and emotional capacity to alter present values of growth and avariciousness. It's a problem of society growing beyond its means, in terms of natural resources, ethics, trust, political structure, and the economic system.

The demonstrators are protesting to highlight the inequality and unfairness of our ruling system, whether it is in liberal democracies in Europe, repressive regimes in China and Russia, brutal dictatorships in Latin America, or corruption in Africa. People know the injustice but not what to do about it. They are enraged by the sheer cheek the 1% dole out at the expense of the 99%, which is establishing a culture of continuing protest. From the Arab Spring, through the Anti-Capitalist sit-ins, to the violent street fights in Africa, to the yellow vests' roadblocks in Europe, to the anti-fracking groups gluing their hands to railings, Extinction Rebellion is spreading around the globe, and school children are on strike. The refugees fleeing war, persecution, environmental degradation, and sheer poverty, cannot be fobbed off with kind words of 'we can take a % of refugees, but the rest...'. This will not do; these protests and migrations are never settled, only deferred, as they build resentment and store frustration, to be let out again in future struggles.

None of this is new. Historians can take us back thousands of years to visit similar stories of outrage and rebellion. The difference today is the scale of the outrage and the extent of the cause of anger; it's global, interconnected, and existential. Instead of spending time learning, enjoying, working, and living, young people the world over are in the streets being teargassed, beaten up, shot at, and in some cases killed. They are enraged with the cockeyed system of economy, government, and businesses in that order, leading to climate catastrophe, inequality, and mass anxiety.

It's only in the last 30 years that a dominant economic system has become global, in the sense that transaction takes a split second. It has become a Goliath. When capitalism stood by our sides, it could be accommodated. It was a bit unfair, but life was still good; fresh air, good quality sufficient food, safe environments, and many things more predictable than is the case now.

The capitalist system has merit to it – freedom of action, relative supportive environment, and material resources galore – but when it becomes excessive, dismissive, and influential, the liberal economic model we use gets abusive in the way it treats employees, customers, and the finite natural world. Economic liberalism has reached its limit of acceptability. The customer is no longer always right; corporations have been given the legal right to prevent employee representatives from forming trade unions. They have been denied the right to collective bargaining. And the environment is free to those who have the means to exploit it the most. The individual element of economic liberalism has turned from being the driver of innovation and economic growth to being anti-competitive and fearing innovation.

National governments, WTO, trade unions, consumers, and even protest and agitation will not prevail against or offer any counterbalance to, the combined might of monopolistic corporatism. In the long term, this unhealthy and unequal state of affairs will damage everyone and everything. There is a need for a realistic and regenerative alternative. Social Enterprise is one such counterbalance that provides a fair and more just way of running a business that fulfils our basic human rights and protects the environment.

Social Enterprise, at a macroeconomic level, maintains much of the market economy of free and equal trade, pays the same taxes as corporate business, is guided by the same laws and policies, operates competitively, and provides income and livelihoods for its members. At the microeconomic level, Social Enterprise overcomes the inequality caused by monopolistic practices and exclusive asset ownership, and counters the danger of civil society being reduced to no more than labour for hire and customers to purchase the goods and services.

Social Enterprise represents the creative destruction of corporate greed with a practical replacement that over many years has proven to be robust and equitable. It operates within a free trade environment, but changes the relationship between labour and capital. From capital hiring and controlling labour, to labour hiring and controlling capital. It does this through being owned by its workforce, its community, and in some cases, by its customers. Both the workforce and communities have a completely different way of seeing the purpose and objectives of trade – as a mature and modern method to enhance their families, communities, and the environment. Social Enterprise invests in social and environmental good practice, is innovative in its commercial trade, radically changes the microeconomic environment for co-owners and their families, local communities, and at the macroeconomic level, the environment and society.

11.1 A call for Action

To respond to the current need for change in economic structures, the social malaise affecting populations, climatic crises, will require the entire world working together. But, with the political hegemony in every country protecting minority vested interests, this seems unlikely. As usual, people on the ground will have to voluntarily do the heavy lifting to get new political arrangement that protects the vast majority of people's interest. Based in the UK and witnessing the stupidity of Brexit, I am fully aware of the difficulty of a united world. But because the global economy is now so prevalent and so many of us are in some way part of it, we have to think and act globally and locally at the same time. Any response must be local and global, and as Social Enterprise is a worldwide phenomenon, it is well placed to be part of any worldwide movement towards a regenerative approach in economics, society, and the natural world.

Time is not on our side. If we do continue as we are, the mounting problems will envelop us in an array of increasingly insolvable issues. The protesting and demonstrations will, and should, continue, as we can't trust the media to inform the public. So the on-the-street, non-violent protest is all that is available. At the same time, now, we need also to be creative and proactive, and those few aware, conscientious politicians who are in positions of influence must get involved and take action.

Social Enterprises can act as catalysts for scaling up alternative and fair commercial ventures. To do so, they need favourable conditions; these can be established through policies targeted to their needs during their scaling trajectory. Significant space exists for new policy actions that inspire and help equality and environmental responsibility scale up the impact these actions have on society and the planet.

Social Enterprise is one such way that people, groups, and politicians can work together in forming alternative structural systems to re-direct our focus towards regenerative and equality approaches.

The way forward:

Formulate

Form a worldwide group to formulate, promote, and enact a Social Enterprise Act, model rules, Social Accounting and Audit procedure, and the necessary education and support mechanisms. This can be done by using the Social Enterprise definition described in this publication as the basis for an international Social Enterprise definition. This is easy to organise, as most agencies supporting Social Enterprise already have a similar definition, and will only need to amend theirs slightly to include all the elements. Also, the agencies are part of international networks already connected to this idea, and able to engage in discussions and debates within existing communication channels.

Agree

Agree a Social Enterprise definition around the six principles stated in chapter 6 of this publication. Draft a Social Enterprise Company Act that is accompanied by a set of model rules and guidance on registration procedures. Agree the Social Accounting and Audit method that fulfils the regenerative approach and triple bottom line principles. This needs to be accepted by the Generally Accepted Accounting Practice (GAAP) and equivalent accounting standards in individual countries. Formulate a set of module rules to accompany the Social Enterprise Act, and have them registered with an appropriate agency responsible for registering Social Enterprises.

Embed

The Social Enterprise Act, model rules, and the Social Accounting and Audit system, can apply to different types of Social Enterprises, such as community enterprises, commercial credit facilities, housing organisations, trading enterprises, and not-for-profit structures. The worldwide group needs to develop a programme of embedding the subject of Social Enterprise in education institutes, public procurement bodies, trade unions, business advice agencies, financial institution, and educational and research bodies, as well as to prepare a range of educational courses for Social Enterprise, ranging from modules for secondary schools to Master diploma courses and PhD subjects at University level.

Network

The worldwide group should negotiate with international bodies, WTO, regional and international banks, UN Agencies, Regional Trade Blocks, and international development organisations, to include Social Enterprise in their policies and services. In the short to medium timescale, create favourable tax incentives for people to set up and operate Social Enterprise. The savings the State makes from Social Enterprise social and environmental investment will offset the cost of tax incentives they provide. Cost savings are generated by Social Enterprise paying higher wages and reduced State aid to low-paid workers, lower costs for a clean environment, and social services supporting people with disabilities and mental stress. Develop research facilities within higher education institutes to enable researchers to investigate Social Enterprise organisation, financing, macroeconomics, asset transfer, and asset lock methods, democratic governance, and group ownership systems. Encourage national government and local authorities to use social procurement clauses and reserved contracts to open up market opportunities for Social Enterprises.

Engage conventional businesses and corporations by providing them with incentives to adopt socially responsible procurement processes. These should provide Social Enterprises with access to an almost unexploited market, and create fertile ground for further scaling. Accompany Social Enterprises' scaling trajectory with tailored (including hybrid) finance, and support the creation of intermediaries that connect them with investors and render them investment ready. Raising awareness is indispensable for scaling impact, and has multiple benefits for

Social Enterprises. Policies and initiatives such as campaigns, awards, labels, and media exposure, not only enhance Social Enterprises' visibility – which can help them generate resources – but also inspire others to replicate their models.

The planet is bursting at the seams, and a few examples of kindness, Sustainable Development Goals, and social mission, is insufficient to overcome the multiple problems facing the world. As we know well, successful, positive societal change includes legal, technical, financial, and human elements working together, reinforcing each other to achieve structural, lasting, positive change. Only once a change has been structurally embedded can it last and withstand the inevitable criticism from vested interests. Social Enterprise without common ownership is missing the point, and Social Enterprise without structural social and environmental practical action is misleading. Social Enterprise comprised of the six values and principles represents an integrated and substantial lasting change process for the better. But it must be enshrined in law as the Social Enterprise Act of Parliament, to guarantee a genuinely open and valuable means for humanity and the planet to prosper.